Rita

Building Consensus:

Conflict and Unity

Monteze M. Snyder

With

Cheryl Gibbs
Susan A. Hillmann
Trayce N. Peterson
Joanna Schofield
George H. Watson

EARLHAM

Earlham Quaker Foundations of Leadership Program
Earlham College, Drawer 97
801 National Road West
Richmond, IN 47374-4095
Phone: 765/983-1426
Fax: 765/983-1207
Consensus website: www.earlham.edu/~consense

ISBN #1-879117-09-6

Contents

Acknowledgments

This book reflects our experience in working in an institution that uses consensus-building processes and consensus decision-making and in teaching about 2,500 people to work with consensus-building and decision-making in a variety of contexts. The form of consensus described in our work draws heavily on the resources for decision-making in the Religious Society of Friends (Quakers; see Chapter 11). Many workshop participants told us that the underlying values and processes for decision-making drawn from Quaker practice could be used in their companies, service organizations, schools, and families. We appreciate the insights of workshop participants, who told us they benefitted from using consensus-building practices even when the final decision on an issue was made by *Robert's Rules of Order* or an executive; that feedback influenced the structure of this book. Fatema Mernissi and leaders of the emerging non-governmental organizations in Morocco reminded us that this shared decision-making approach is crucial for creating and sustaining commitment in these fragile organizations that are so crucial for democratic development; our work with them helped us see the cross-cultural applications of consensus decision-making more clearly.

Our training activities and development of these materials were made possible by a generous grant from the W. K. Kellogg Foundation of Battle Creek, Michigan. We especially appreciate the encouragement and support of John C. Burkhardt and Mary Lynn Falbe of the Foundation, who challenged us to discover how a Quaker-based form of consensus would be useful in a variety of settings.

We gratefully acknowledge the contributions of numerous colleagues, students and other Friends at Earlham and elsewhere in the development of this book. Randall and Alice Shrock were instrumental in initiating this work. We drew on countless documents in the Quaker Archives of Earlham College that were carefully identified for us by Ellen Stanley. Nelson Bingham, Marya Bower, Len Clark, Caroline Estes, Margaret Lechner, Diana Punzo, Bill Remmes, and Jerry Woolpy contributed draft material and other inputs to the text. Others helped us frame the content of this manual through thoughtful discussion: Stephanie Crumley-Effinger, RitaLinda D'Andrea, Mary Ann Downey, Art Fink, Paul Lacey, Don McNemar, Jay Marshall, Laura Melly, Gene Mills, John Punshon, Gil White, and Peter Woodrow. We have also benefitted from feedback from others who used earlier versions of these materials to present workshops: Nakia Barnett, Fran Berry, Nelson Bingham, Lincoln Blake, Lisbeth Borie, Len Clark, Mary Ann Downey, Beth Duckles, David Gerth, Daniel Hunter, Ryan Irwin, Rick Jurasek, Tom Kirk, Rinn Lawson, Margaret Lechner, Theresa Ludwig, Yazeed Moor, Don McNemar, George Nuñez, Sara Penhale, Marco Rankin, Sofie Richardson, Suzannah Mullin Schmitz, Liz Soitsman, Larry Spears, Elizabeth Stark, Andy Verostek, Jonas Walker, Dory Weiss, Peter Woodrow, and Cecelia Yocum. Our collaboration with Russ Barenburg, Bart Brammer, Mike Herron, and Jerry Wallace at Saturn Corporation stimulated our thinking and sharpened our language.

Our efforts to use the materials in as many different settings as possible were supported by Aletha Stahl, Diya AlaEdeen, and Musa Khalidi, who translated the materials into French and Arabic for us.

We are grateful to Richmond, Indiana, Mayor Dennis Andrews and Earlham colleagues Evan Farber, Paul Lacey, Sara Penhale, and John Punshon for their efficient and thorough final review of the book before it went to press.

Melanie Weidner Watson receives our heartfelt thanks for her visual representation of the essence of consensus-building that appears on our cover.

The writings of Friends provided essential background and history on Quaker practice; these are noted in Chapter 11. Our understanding and appreciation of consensus-building and consensus decision-making has been profoundly influenced by our respective participation in Quaker meetings and Quaker-based organizations over the years. These experiences have been powerful teachers.

Earlham Quaker Foundations of Leadership Program staff:

Monteze M. Snyder
Joanna Schofield
Trayce M. Peterson
Susan A. Hillmann

Chapter 1
Consensus — A Different Approach

Introduction

This book is intended for use by people who are using or considering using consensus processes in their workplaces, community organizations, schools, families or other social settings. A group or team may use *consensus-building* processes to strengthen its understanding of relevant concerns and potential consequences even when a decision will ultimately be made by the boss or by a final vote. A wide variety of organizations use *consensus decision-making* processes for some or many of their decisions, ranging from strategic planning groups of corporations and production teams in the automotive and motorcycle industries to grass roots social action groups and natural resources planning councils (Susskind, McKearnan, & Thomas-Larner, 1999; Gastil, 1993; Gerber, 1992).

Consensus Is a Learning Process

Most of us are well-schooled in deciding by majority rule or having a boss decide. But we've had less practice in seeking the common good together, listening to different voices, weaving together common ideas and concerns, agreeing on a decision that reflects what is good for the group at that time, and taking responsibility collectively for the decision and its consequences. Learning to approach decision-making this way takes practice. Coaching or training by someone with experience in using consensus helps.

<u>Why</u> Use Consensus-Building and Decision-Making

Consensus-building emphasizes cooperation in sharing information and airing differences, which provides an opportunity for new ideas to emerge. It also affects how members experience the process and the value of their contributions. Consensus-building reminds us that we share a common humanity, even with our differences.

Perceptions of fairness of the decision-making process often vary according to whether one's views were heard or considered. It is important that members understand that their viewpoints have been considered without requiring that others agree with them. Consensus-building establishes underlying attitudes and provides clear practices for encouraging consideration of different views, thereby strengthening the sense of fairness. This is particularly important in diverse groups or groups with some members whose voices are seldom heard.

trust building, confidence building

Broader commitment and acceptance of decisions may be created and then strengthened through consensus-building. When the views of members were considered in management teams in a Fortune 500 company, commitment to the decision, attachment to the group, and trust in the leadership were strengthened (Korsgaard, Schweiger, & Sapienza, 1995). Sometimes, the decision has broader acceptance if it is made by consensus. When top level executives at AT&T were divided and at a standstill, they convened task forces and called on Quaker Robert Greenleaf, who built consensus in these groups and worked with them to reach consensus decisions. "A task force report that has a minority report attached to it is really of very little value. Unless it has complete agreement, it really doesn't settle much. It leaves the matter still open where it was at the start" (Greenleaf, 1987). When the task forces reached hard-won agreement, the executives accepted the results of the groups' deliberations.

Consensus processes create a level of confidence that helps people bear the costs of change, which typically come before the benefits. In the course of building consensus, major challenges that might emerge during implementation of various decision options are often identified, reducing the surprises that can undercut effective implementation. When the group makes the decision by consensus, the confidence may be even stronger, and implementation may be quicker and more effective.

Capacity for ongoing cooperation, collaboration and co-ownership are developed through consensus-building and decision-making. Members are encouraged to see the decisions and the work of the organization as theirs, not just the responsibility of those in charge. The more practice a group has in building agreement, the more strength it has for meeting the challenges of the next decision-making situation.

What Consensus Processes Look Like: Three Examples from Practice

• In a multinational automotive firm, consensus-building processes helped people overcome the low level of trust that existed after massive layoffs. The diverse staff of the publications and technical support unit began by making decisions together about small matters. Then they initiated cross-functional teams. Now they negotiate job sharing. Customer satisfaction, productivity and job satisfaction have improved. They also work differently now. The facilitators for their meetings are not the managers in charge of the unit. Dissent is considered important to making quality decisions. Throughout the process, an external consultant coaches the group and raises key questions about the process. The consultant also helps a perpetually dissenting member sort out the personal and organizational issues underlying his opposition.

unity

• The board of directors of a nonprofit school decided to adopt the attitudes and practices that help build consensus, while keeping a provision that required matters of legal consequence to be decided by a vote that would be documented in the minutes. They continued to vote on decisions regarding matters such as mortgages and budgets, but they did so after a discussion process that usually resulted in unity. In one controversial decision, the

How Consensus Works: An Overview

The consensus process is like a funnel — wide open at the outset to allow for broad participation, then gradually narrowing as it channels the content towards a preliminary summary in consensus building (Stage 1). If the group uses consensus decision-making, a series of summaries leads toward a decision (Stage 2).

Stage 1: Consensus-Building

1. Working groups, committees, or individuals with relevant background information circulate documents before the meeting. Members do their homework in advance.

2. The meeting opens according to the group's usual practice. Some groups use a period of silence to permit everyone to reflect on their common purpose and to prepare for working together.

3. The facilitator or clerk identifies a specific agenda item. Individuals or the group in charge of providing the relevant information summarize the key issues.

4. With a pause between speakers, members are recognized by the facilitator or clerk to contribute their concerns, ideas and information to the group as a whole. The facilitator or clerk stays neutral about the issue.

5. No motions are made. The facilitator or clerk periodically summarizes the discussion without naming anyone, reflecting common concerns and issues of difference. This summary may be acknowledged by the group as a reflection of their deliberations and handed over to the ultimate decision-maker, or the group may proceed to Stage 2 to reach a decision by consensus.

Stage 2: Consensus Decision-Making

6. Steps 4 and 5 continue until a decision becomes clearer.

7. The facilitator or clerk identifies what appears to be the emerging decision and asks for unresolved concerns. If necessary, the stated decision is revised to more adequately reflect the group's conclusion.

8. The facilitator or clerk asks for approval. The approved decision is announced.

The group has made the decision by consensus.

responsibility

board decided in unity to turn the decision over to a committee without anticipating all of the consequences of that choice. Even when unintended consequences emerged later, the board did not engage in blaming the committee but rather viewed the decision — even with its unintended consequences — as the responsibility of the whole group.

- The supply of freshwater is one of the major concerns in the complex Middle East conflict. Gilbert White, Quaker and noted geographer, chaired a study committee that was the first collaborative effort of scientists from Israel, Jordan, the Palestinian Authority, the United States, and Canada. Using consensus, the committee was able to agree upon a report that outlined a plan of how Israel, Jordan and the Palestinian Authority could work together to protect and conserve water ecosystems in the region for use now and for future generations.

This Manual's Approach to Consensus

Deciding by consensus has been part of the organizational and political life of many groups for centuries (Mansbridge, 1980). Although the approach presented in this manual has much in common with other consensus approaches, it is unique in that it draws on the religious method used for decision-making by the Religious Society of Friends (Quakers) for almost 350 years.

Participants from a wide variety of faith backgrounds in our workshops have indicated that the values and practices of this approach have been useful to them, regardless of their own religious or spiritual beliefs. Adapted from the Quaker practice, the consensus process can be effective in any group whose members share hopes and beliefs about their ability to engage in collective action for the common good. The examples given earlier in this chapter were based on the form of consensus used by Friends. Although Quaker-based consensus has been used in groups as large as 600, this manual is written primarily for groups up to 100; we have had direct experience using it in groups this size.

Some features of Quaker-based consensus practices include:

- The process is grounded in beliefs and values that consider the relationship of individuals and the group in the search for truth and good decisions.

- It is a process for seeking the truth in unity, not necessarily unanimity.

- Quaker-based consensus allows for several forms of dissent. Respect for an individual's own truth is held in tension with the mutual responsibility of each member of the group. While some other models assume that there is no systematic consideration of differences in consensus, Quaker-based consensus practices assume that constructive engagement of differences and dissent are integral to the process.

- A facilitator or clerk, who in business or other organizational settings is usually not the executive or person in charge, plays a key role in coordinating the process.

The attitudes, practices and basic approaches for dealing with differences in consensus-building or decision-making are presented in Chapters 2-4. Chapter 5 describes the process of consensus decision-making. Chapter 6 explores the work of the clerk or facilitator. This chapter will be helpful for facilitators of consensus-building efforts and provides detailed guidance for facilitating or clerking consensus decision-making meetings. For groups that choose to make decisions by consensus, Chapters 7-9 provide guidance for setting the agenda, taking minutes, and handling dissent. Chapter 10 compares consensus decision-making with two other approaches and provides a rationale for the use of consensus decision-making in certain situations. It also provides a framework for considering consensus-building as part of other decision-making processes. Those interested in a brief introduction to the use of consensus by Quakers are invited to read Chapter 11, which also includes a list of basic resources from the Quaker literature on consensus that provided the published basis for our work. The appendices include additional tools for using consensus, including a checklist for assessing consensus practice (Appendix A) and a form for evaluating group dynamics and subgroup influence (Appendix B). Although we have more experience with consensus practice that is face-to-face and find this format to be indispensable for many decisions, we also offer guidelines for use of e-mail in the consensus process (Appendix C).

Additional materials about consensus-building and consensus decision-making and resources for training are available on the Internet website at www.earlham.edu/~consense.

Chapter 2
Attitudes that Set the Stage for Consensus-Building

what about consensus + INTASC?

Introduction

Our attitudes about working in groups are shaped first by our interactions with our families, then by our activities with childhood friends, classmates and teachers, and eventually by the people we know at work and in other group settings. These interactions cause us to develop theories and beliefs about how groups function, who influences decisions, and whether the decision-making process and results suit us.

Those theories and beliefs, in turn, form the basis for attitudes that influence how we work in groups. We may make a habit of deferring to or being suspicious of people who are in positions of authority or who have special expertise. We may view group consensus-building as either beneficial or inefficient, which may influence how carefully and patiently we listen to other group members. Or we may believe that our views are either more or less important than those of others, which may influence how much, or even if, we speak.

I like that

Teachers can cause, and/or have to deal with this

The consensus approach gives us an opportunity to assess and sometimes recast our beliefs and attitudes about power and authority. The goal of employing consensus-building techniques is to bring out the best thinking of any group about how to deal with shared concerns. Our attitudes about one another and about our responsibility to the whole group affect how well we are able to reach that goal.

Different Lights — One Picture

Imagine we are taken to a room we have never seen. It is the middle of the night and there are no overhead lights on in the room. As a group, we are assigned the task of drawing an accurate picture of this room. We have different kinds of lights to use to be able to see the room: some of us have little penlights for seeing details; some of us have searchlights for seeing large parts of the room; some of us have strobe lights for catching movement. Using the pieces of information we each capture by shining our different lights, we must agree upon a description of the room.

Determining the "right" decision is often like this. Each of us has a different way of seeing things, and we can benefit as a group by sharing our perspectives. When we are uncertain about the outcomes and consequences of our choices, we are often designing in the dark. We never know which light might provide crucial insight.

Consensus-Building Attitudes

Consensus-building creates an atmosphere in which group members have the opportunity to share information, discuss differences, learn from each other, and collectively create new ideas. Adopting the following attitudes are extremely helpful when building consensus within a group.

Trust that by putting our heads and hearts together, we can identify common ground and ways of moving forward that address the concerns of the group.

Consensus-building encourages piecing together various individuals' suggestions, which then are reworked as new ideas are added during the discussion. The resulting solution is usually better and more creative than any one person's idea. Getting to that better idea, however, often requires patience and trust, especially when it may seem that the discussion is moving very slowly. Mutual accountability and careful discernment of crucial issues are essential to building consensus within a group. Trust is usually tentative when a group is just beginning to work together. As the group experiences the results of successful consensus process, trust grows. When making decisions by consensus, the group takes collective responsibility for its decisions and the outcome of those decisions.

From Win-Lose to Learn-Learn

Consensus-building emphasizes learning rather than winning. Only by intentionally replacing preconceived notions with authentic listening and learning will you be able to participate fully in consensus-building.

- Learn from each other, regardless of expertise or position. Try to understand what matters to others and why.

- Learn to seek greater clarity about the reasons for and conditions of various alternatives to make the best decision.

- Learn to be patient with each other and with the process. With successful practice, groups gradually develop the capacity to make better decisions more quickly.

Place a high value on acting in unity.

V. important

This form of consensus distinguishes between unity and unanimity. Unanimity implies that everyone agrees with a particular solution. Unity allows for one or more members of a group to disagree with a decision, yet support it because they believe it to be in the best interest of the group at that time, given the feasible options.

Regard all ideas as the property of the group.

Once ideas are put forward, think of them as the property of the group rather than as ideas associated with specific people. When offering an idea, give it freely, with the expectation that it can be useful to the group in a variety of ways — even if it does not survive in its original form. Giving the whole group ownership of ideas makes it easier to change or combine them or to set them aside as the group works to draw together the best ideas into a decision. It also reduces power struggles over specific suggestions. Consensus-building emphasizes learning rather than winning.

this goes for teachers!

★ Be open to the possibility that the best solution for the group may not be the one you personally prefer.

The consensus process is designed to help the group achieve its goals and shared mission, and to build group trust and commitment over an extended period of time. As we participate in the process, it is helpful to be united by the belief that when the group achieves its goals, we as individuals also benefit. To achieve this shared mission, some of us may need to set aside certain personal preferences, goals and desires. We do this not by negotiating or compromising, but by consciously choosing to realign our goals and desires to fit with those of the group.

Respect each person as important to the process.

In the consensus process, the unique experience and insight of each person is recognized and valued. We can never be sure who is going to contribute a crucial element to the discussion. Sometimes even the simplest

what's your def. of community. community good - does that fit

> ### Core Quaker Beliefs that Influence the Development of Consensus-Building Attitudes
>
> - There is that of God — or, in more secular terms, there is the will and power to do [good] — in everyone. Each of us can experience this part of the divine, and our experience is an important part of deciding what actions are right for us in a group or community.
>
> - All people are equal in the eyes of God and thus are entitled to equal respect.
>
> - No one has the whole truth. The sharing of individual understanding of truth is an important part of any consensus-building process.

question or comment can turn the process in a constructive direction. Unless each contribution is respectfully considered, the best solution may not be achieved. It is not necessary, however, for each individual to speak; sometimes one person may voice the concerns shared by several others.

Maintain self-confidence and respect for yourself.

Think abt. contrast w/ voting scenarios

Do not underestimate the importance of your participation. Your contribution may take many forms: you may ask a question, voice a concern, provide constructive criticism of an idea, or clarify an important connection between ideas that have been offered by others. Trust that your unique perspective is needed by the group. Be attentive to your insights and speak honestly when you have something to share.

Remain open to new insights and be willing to modify your thinking.

Do not become overly attached to or invested in an idea — your own or someone else's — as it is first described. Be open to how the idea may be improved. Try not to take suggested changes or criticisms as challenges to you or other individuals who proposed the idea. At the heart of building consensus is the understanding that we can learn from one another as we seek the solution that is best for all.

Keep status, expertise, and personal feelings in perspective when considering someone's ideas.

Concentrate more on the idea or the suggestion than on the person who offers it. Don't give undue weight to the opinions of people in positions of authority, and don't underestimate the value of the contributions of others. Stay focused on the idea, rather than on its source.

Value the constructive aspects of disagreement.

Value disagreement as something that can help generate more creative solutions. When we listen carefully to differing points of view and understand the values behind them, we can discover legitimate concerns or weaknesses that should be addressed. This discovery can save us from making costly mistakes. It also can help us resolve the disagreement by identifying common ground. Responding with respect to people who have different views increases trust and strengthens the group. When groups and individual members do not establish a culture that permits working with divergent viewpoints, the risk of false agreement, bad decisions, and ongoing covert conflict is higher (Harvey, 1988).

Chapter 3
Practices that Support Consensus-Building

Introduction

The core beliefs and attitudes discussed in the previous chapter are brought to life in the behaviors and practices used in consensus-building. Although specialized expertise and experience are valued in consensus-building and decision-making, crucial insights may come from a variety of people. Because approaches based on expertise and authority are much more common in today's organizations, many of us feel a bit awkward when we first participate in a consensus process. Using the practices described below can help you make a smooth transition to consensus.

Practices that Support Consensus

Following is an overview of the basic guidelines for participating more meaningfully in the consensus-building process. Use the checklist at the end of the chapter to discover which specific behaviors you do well and which ones are difficult for you. Consciously working to improve how you participate can increase the quality of both the consensus process itself and the resulting decision.

Prepare the meeting space.

Someone should be charged with the task of preparing the meeting space. This person may be the facilitator or clerk, a convener, a chairperson, or someone else willing to accept the responsibility. Since the ambiance of the meeting space can affect how well group members work together, the room should be arranged in such a way that is conducive to consensus-building. Consider the space of the room, the lighting, the temperature, the amount of privacy, space for smaller groups to meet, and the materials needed (for example, flip chart, markers, etc.). Arrange the tables and chairs according to the composition and nature of your group. For a small group, it is preferable to have a table for the clerks and chairs for the group members set up in a circle or an oval. For a larger group, make sure that the seating arrangement allows everyone to hear each other. You might want to consider using microphones.

Classroom environment

Prepare for the meeting.

If documents or reports have been circulated before the meeting, read them. Reading reports and other background information relevant to the discussion before the meeting allows for more time during the meeting to discuss the issue and to clarify concerns. If you know in advance what issues will be considered at the meeting, spend some time reflecting on the views you will carry into the meeting. Try to become clear about your views and why you hold them. At the same time, remember to be open to new ideas and alternative outcomes. If you have gaps in your knowledge or understanding of the matter, gather information or find other ways to fill the gaps. Notify the facilitator or clerk if you have information that may be valuable to the group. It might be important to give people time to consider the information in advance, or allow time during the meeting for you to present it to the group. Arrive a few minutes early in order to focus on the task at hand and mentally prepare yourself for participating in a group effort.

Establish ground rules for working together.

Groups work better when everyone knows the rules of the game and follows them. Take time to establish ground rules that meet the needs of your particular group. The Consensus Practices Checklist (Appendix A) is useful for developing these ground rules.

During the meeting, listen carefully and considerately to others.

Try to identify the underlying need, interest, or concern of a position expressed by another member of the group. Ask for clarification or more information when needed. When you find yourself resisting a position, ask yourself, "Why does this concern or idea matter to that person?" Avoid devaluing someone's ideas because you dislike that person or don't trust their motivation. Do not put your hand up or interrupt while others are speaking.

Provide pauses between speakers to allow thoughts to settle.

Pausing between speakers frames each person's comments in silence that allows for reflection. This creates mental space for more thoughtful deliberation and discussion. Silence also encourages people to listen to each speaker without simultaneously thinking of what they wish to say in response.

If you feel moved to speak, think first.

It isn't necessary for everyone to speak, especially if your concern or idea has already been voiced by someone else. If you have a new contribution to make, think before you speak. Is what you are going to say meant for the whole group to hear, or just for yourself, or for a seemingly confused person who spoke earlier? Will what you want to say forward the flow of conversation? Are you clear about what you want to say? Can you express your views directly, calmly and respectfully? When you have considered these questions and feel you are ready to speak, ask for recognition from the facilitator or clerk.

Make your point to the group as a whole, then allow others to speak.

If you have information that can help the group gain greater clarity about the problem or proposed solutions, be sure to offer it. When speaking, be brief and to the point. Rather than repeating a statement or position already voiced, consider saying, "X (person's name) has spoken my mind." Speak only once on a topic until others have been heard. Avoid having back and forth dialogue between individuals. Don't be surprised if remarks made after you speak don't necessarily respond or refer to what you said.

Welcome creative transformations of ideas.

Recognize that all ideas are the property of the group, subject to revision and transformation. Don't become overly attached to a specific proposal. If new information or insights suggest a better way to proceed, it is best to set aside ideas that no longer work. In the course of discussion, if you discover that a concern you raised earlier is no longer central to the group's deliberation, consider withdrawing it so that the group can move on to points that need further work.

Be aware of how your identity and background impact your influence in the group.

In ongoing groups the pattern of behavior by those who are most comfortable or experienced may pose challenges for the group's effectiveness. Those who are most comfortable are often unaware of the way in which their behaviors influence the involvement of newcomers or other marginalized groups. In addition to considering the following queries, the group may be helped by using the Group Dynamics Evaluation Form found in the Appendix B.

Queries for Participating Members

Queries have long been used by Quakers as a way to reflect upon the underlying bases of their actions, behaviors, and thoughts. Using thought-provoking questions encourages participants to examine their lives carefully without having to follow a given set of rigid rules. Following is a set of queries to help established group members evaluate how they interact with other members, and a set to encourage participation of newcomers.

Queries for Established Members of a Group

- Have I encouraged the members who are newcomers, seldom-heard, categorized, and marginalized — including those with whom I might not be in agreement — to explore their concerns and ideas with me or with the facilitator or clerk outside of the meeting?

- Have I respectfully shared background information on the problem that might not be known to newcomers or marginalized members?

- Do my relationships outside of the meeting with newcomers or marginalized members encourage them to participate in the community?

- After a meeting, do I acknowledge the contributions of newcomers or others who have spoken as a way of acknowledging that they have been heard and of encouraging them to continue participating?

Queries for Newcomers to a Group

- Do I recognize when and how I may contribute to addressing the issue at hand — by asking a clarifying question, providing data, or offering a perspective that is important in defining the problem or finding a solution?

- Do I accept both my right and my responsibility to speak about the issues before the group, regardless of the personal issues that I may have?

- Is my heart pounding in a way that signals me that I am compelled to share my viewpoint, or is this a time when I need to speak on a more minor point that gives me practice in participating?

- Do I understand that there probably will be no response in the meeting to what I have said or recognition of the ideas I put forth as mine, but this does not mean that my contribution has been ignored?

- Do I recognize that different institutions and groups have a common language that may be different from mine? Have I identified someone whom I trust to ask for translation or explanation?

- If I have concerns about negative consequences of offering my contribution, have I realistically assessed the risk as well as the likelihood of negative consequences for this action? Can I ask a trusted senior member of the organization to help me think through the risks and likelihood of negative consequences for making the kind of statement I feel I should make?

- While I am aware that all have equal rights and responsibilities to participate in shaping the decision, do I also recognize the paradox that some people's views may be accorded special consideration because they are regarded as having have special wisdom or experience? (Note: This consideration may not be based on position power.)

Checklist For Consensus-Building Behavior

*Put a **plus (+)** next to 2-3 items in the list below that you think you do easily and well. Mark those that you find more challenging with an **asterisk (*)**. Indicate those that seem unclear or confusing with a **question mark (?)**.*

___ Stay focused on the good of the group and not just on my own preferences.

Accept that disagreement can be normal and useful.

Listen actively and accurately.

___ Try to understand *why* a concern or idea matters to a particluar person or what the underlying concern really is.

Use body language and facial expressions that show I am listening and consider others to be reasonable people.

Avoid negative feelings (anger, frustration or criticism) towards an individual.

Treat differences in ideas and strategies respectfully.

Ask for recognition to speak only after the person speaking has finished.

Leave silence between speakers.

Put forth information in a well-organized, well-reasoned way.

Speak only once on a topic until other members have spoken.

Address the group rather than a specific person so that there is no debate between individuals.

Respectfully ask others for their ideas or opinions, facts, or other information to back up their ideas.

Express ideas and opinions other than those that have already been heard.

Offer praise or appreciation for ideas expressed by others.

Recognize particular expertise of others.

Build on other ideas or comments to propose a conclusion or new direction.

Summarize the discussion, including points of agreement and difference.

Withdraw earlier statements of concern when new information or insights suggest a better way forward.

Chapter 4
When We Disagree

Introduction

Disagreement is part of the consensus process, and experience shows that it often leads to new and better solutions. Group members can draw on a variety of processes to work toward consensus when disagreement arises. These processes work whether the disagreement consists of mild differences of opinion, heated conflict, or anything in between. Other techniques of conflict resolution may also be used.

The Pause that Refreshes

A county school board in Indiana was locked in contentious battle. At the peak of the conflict, a board member asked if the group could take a moment of silence to allow the group to return to a sense of its common humanity and purpose. When the discussion resumed, it was with a new tone of respect for the views of others.

When Disagreement Occurs

Disagreement often produces tension between group members. Reminding yourself that disagreements are a normal part of group discussion can help you manage your anxiety. During a meeting in which disagreement arises, the group as a whole should:

- Provide opportunities for everyone to share and receive information, and to present divergent viewpoints.

- Reinforce the use of pauses between speakers and other techniques of active listening with the intent of understanding the essential concerns and ideas that are present in differing viewpoints.

- Support participants — particularly those who are in disagreement — as they seek greater understanding of their own concerns.

- Identify the issues that have been raised, to summarize the points of agreement and disagreement, to suggest alternatives and to move the discussion along. If participants hear their viewpoints represented in others' statements, they should affirm the statements. If not, they should restate or clarify the aspects of their views that have been omitted.

- Enter into a few moments of silence if the discussion becomes so heated that members are having difficulty listening to each other. Remind members that the purpose of pausing is to restore a sense of group unity and to reflect upon the group's intent to reach agreement.

- Look for an alternative that no one has yet mentioned which might address the group's goals and concerns.

- Encourage discussion of the issue during breaks — particularly among those who disagree.

Tips for Active Listening

Considering the following questions can help you better understand other group members whose positions differ from yours:

- Do I really want to reach agreement?

- Am I really listening well, regardless of who is speaking?

- Have I been truly open to considering others' ideas and suggestions?

- Can I articulate the concerns of the differing position in a way that the speaker would agree that I had listened well?

- Have we provided opportunities for everyone to share and receive information and to present divergent viewpoints?

When Disagreement Persists

When dealing with disagreement, it is important to remember that forming coalitions and factions usually deepens the disagreement to the point of conflict and causes the opposing "sides" to dig in their heels. Mounting support for a particular position is discouraged in the consensus-building process.

If disagreement persists, the group could choose to do one or more of the following actions:

- Get a clear sense of the level of disagreement. Ask who is uncomfortable with the proposal, who is in agreement with it, and who could live with it.

- Go beyond asking "What are the points of disagreement?" Ask "Why is this a particular concern for someone?" This helps group members identify and understand the underlying concerns.

- Break into small groups to identify the underlying needs and interests.

- Charge small groups with brainstorming new proposals that can be brought back to the large group.

- Brainstorm options of how to move forward. Evaluate these process options to see if they meet the needs and interests of the group.

- Hold the matter over to another meeting, if time permits. This allows time for those who have offered different perspectives to have informal discussion and conflict resolution between them before the next meeting.

- Refer the matter to a formal or an ad hoc committee to explore the issues involved in the decision. The committee should involve those who have divergent viewpoints.

- Hold a special "threshing session" — a meeting to cull out the essential tensions involved in dealing with the matter and to identify underlying concerns.

- Gather together in small, diverse groups expressly *not* to discuss the conflict but rather to refresh the bonds of friendship within the group.

Chapter 5
Deciding by Consensus

Introduction

Making decisions by consensus can be an invigorating experience for a group. The possibility of achieving a deeper level of working together, honoring the insights and concerns of members while moving towards creative, common solutions and decisions can energize a group of people who had given up hope of being able to function well together. Consensus decision-making requires awareness, energy, creativity, patience, and honesty of the facilitator or clerk and group members. This chapter focuses on the mechanics of getting started, aspects of group participation in the process, and elements of consensus decision-making.

Getting Started

Once your group has decided to use the consensus decision-making process, certain elements have to be put in place to begin your work. For those charged with implementing this process, the following information is helpful as you make the transition.

Get a facilitator or clerk for decision-making.

As the person in charge of managing the discussion and framing the solution, the facilitator or clerk must be chosen with great care. It is important that the facilitator or clerk receive training in managing the whole consensus process or at least observe a skilled clerk and have the opportunity for coaching and feedback (See Chapter 6; contact us at the address inside the front cover). A recorder also may be identified to help keep track of the ideas and points of discussion that emerge (See Chapter 8).

Get together.

The facilitator or clerk should review with the group the ground rules for working together. Group members need to embody the attitudes and practices that support consensus-building. Discuss and agree upon additional ground rules necessary for your particular group. The attitudes and practices described in Chapters 2 and 3 are a useful place to begin.

Get clear.

Know the limits of your decision-making powers. Does your group or unit have the authority to decide on this issue? Depending on the problem, find out who has the prerogative to make a recommendation or to decide definitely about this issue.

Get information.

The best decisions can only be made when the group has clear, relevant information and understands what is at stake.

- Who has information about this issue?
- Who has expertise?
- Who has relevant experience?
- Who are the stakeholders who may be affected by potential solutions?
- How will the group get input from these constituencies?
- To whom will the decision or recommendation be reported and how?
- How will information be distributed outside of face-to-face meetings? (See Appendix C.)

Get going — carefully.

Start with fairly simple issues. Give your group time to gain confidence, experience and skill with consensus decision-making before attempting more difficult issues.

Get help.

For inexperienced groups or those with difficulties, appoint an observer to provide feedback on how group members interact during the consensus process. The Consensus Practices Checklist (Appendix A) can be used to give the group feedback. If difficulties persist, it may be necessary for the group to get training from an outside consultant and to confer with others who are experienced with consensus processes. Our web page provides a forum for that purpose.

The Role of Group Members

Successful consensus decision-making is based on group members believing in the process, accepting responsibility for the group's decisions and actions, and participating in the discussion and in the search for unity about a decision. The specific roles listed below are an extension of the attitudes and practices presented in Chapters 2 and 3. Assuming these roles permits you to encourage and support the consensus decision-making process and avoid viewing it as an adversarial process.

- **Team player:** Prepare yourself to influence and to be influenced cooperatively in searching for the right decision for your group. Take your share of responsibility for the group's work. Work to overcome weaknesses and build on strengths.

- **Contributor of ideas:** You are responsible for sharing your ideas, concerns, and points of disagreement with confidence and clarity.

- **Active listener:** Listen attentively to others in a non-judgmental way. Acknowledge the parts of other positions with which you agree. Ensure that the stated decision reflects the corporate understanding and decision.

- **Learner:** Be open to learning from those who have a different perspective than you do. Try to understand individual personalities and how they interact in groups.

- **Problem solver:** Creatively search for the appropriate answers which meet all reasonable objections to the current proposal. Avoid easy acquiescence to apparent group agreement; persist in pursuing a good decision for the group as a whole.

- **Trusting participant:** Trust in the process. Remain positive that your group will reach the best decision for the group.

Elements of Consensus Decision-Making for the Group

The input that you provide is really what consensus decision-making is all about: groups members engage one another around issues and ideas to arrive at a decision that members can support at this time. What you as a group decide is going to have an impact on the organization — hopefully in a positive manner. Several aspects of the decision-making process that are specific to consensus are described below. You will want to keep these in mind as you participate.

Weaving ideas

A metaphor that might be helpful for explaining discussion and the decision-making process is that of weaving. This image is reflected in the figure on page 46. Your group's ideas are the threads that are essential to making the fabric of the decision. If you or other group members have new ideas or concerns but don't share them, there may be holes in the decision. Some threads continue to support the weaving even though other threads cover them. Some threads are only partially visible. Others are interwoven to form a different type of thread. And still others fall by the wayside after consideration. The facilitator or clerk serves as the one who pulls all of these threads into some coherent form. As group members, you test this description against your own understanding of the group's agreement.

Valuing minority opinion

The consensus decision-making process encourages expression of minority opinion. As a group member with a minority point of view you have the responsibility to share your point of view with the group. The information you share may help to stimulate the group's thinking and may address a concern not yet reflected in the discussion. In turn, group members must listen carefully to the information offered to examine whether it is necessary to modify their beliefs in light of new data and insights. Being open to hearing and learning from minority voices changes the direction of the process and influences the final decision.

Sometimes this is reflected directly in a decision made by the group. In other cases, the group may remain clear that the original formulation is right for the group at this time for acceptable reasons.

Sometimes a group is initially unable to come to a clear agreement. In the course of laboring to understand the concerns of a member who sees the situation or desirable solution differently, another group member may offer an alternative solution. Suddenly, it seems that this is the right way to proceed, and the group approves the decision. Groups experienced with consensus decision-making often recount these stories as memorable decision events. This is reflected in the figure on page 47.

Formalizing the decision

At a given point in the discussion, the facilitator or clerk will provide a formulation of the unity that the group has reached. A time of quiet may be necessary for the facilitator or clerk to formulate and articulate the decision. It is important for all group members to listen carefully to the formulation. The facilitator or clerk will ask for approval of the decision under consideration. Speak up if you think that the issue is not yet fully resolved or if the stated formulation does not fully capture the group's conclusion. Discussion continues until the concerns are resolved. The facilitator or clerk may need to offer various revisions of the formulation to accurately reflect the group's decision.

Chapter 6
The Facilitator or Clerk in the Consensus Process

Introduction

The person who leads the consensus decision-making process is called the facilitator or clerk. In Quaker-based organizations and Friends Meetings, the person who convenes the consensus process is called the "clerk of the meeting." Because the modern use of the word "clerk" has connotations that do not reflect the robust leadership role of this position, the term facilitator is often used in other settings. This chapter is written for

> **WANTED: Facilitator/Clerk for Consensus**
>
> Must be able to keep group members focused on learning from each other. Basic qualities include ability to understand and manage group dynamics, and awareness of how cultural patterns and power influence participation. Should be able to appreciate people for their differences. References should verify integrity, courage, and ability to put aside personal viewpoints. Keen sense of humor is a plus.

those of you who are facilitators or clerks. Your job is to recognize common themes of agreement as well as to identify differences and conflicts. You will serve the group by advocating the process of consensus rather than promoting a particular position, including a personal one. If your group is building consensus but making the decision by another process, a clerk or facilitator may still be useful.

In some organizations or groups, the director, chairperson, or executive may be responsible for organizing the meeting and presenting the issues. If you have position power and are going to facilitate meetings, you must be able to be neutral and not take a major role in the substance of the issue. This issue is further explored in Chapter 10.

The challenges of clerking a consensus-building and decision-making meeting can be lessened when you fully understand the scope of your role, have the proper tools for the job, and can draw on the knowledge of experienced clerks. This chapter outlines your role in a consensus meeting. It also suggests techniques for handling difficult situations.

The Role of the Facilitator or Clerk

To serve the group effectively as facilitator or clerk, you must be able to fulfill multiple roles during the consensus process. These roles seem to put you on "center stage" and give you a certain amount of authority and power. You must, however, remember that you really are a servant of your group or organization.

In addition, while you as facilitator or clerk have the overall responsibility of fulfilling these roles, you can only do so completely when members of the group also embody these roles to the best of their ability. Your major roles include:

Essential Qualities of a Clerk

Quaker Robert Greenleaf, founder of the Servant Leadership movement, worked for many years in management research, development and education at AT&T. In addition, he was a consultant for M.I.T., the Ford Foundation, and many other organizations. Greenleaf (1987) affirms that the art of managing a consensus process rests on the clerk's having two very important qualities:

1) Faith in the process. The clerk must have a firm belief that consensus will emerge if worked with long enough and must communicate this belief through manner and facial expressions.

2) Skill of language and ideas. The clerk must be willing to try another set of words and ideas until consensus is found.

These are crucial to the leadership of consensus decision-making.

- **Educating:** Help new people understand what is going on and help other members be more effective participants in the consensus process.

- **Tone setting:** Model attitudes that create an atmosphere in which people will be caring, considerate and respectful of one another.

- **Facilitating:** Manage the process while remaining neutral to the content of issues raised.

- **Nurturing of group members:** Encourage participation of all group members. Also encourage people to use their expertise, talents and abilities.

- **Encouraging acceptance of differences:** Help widen the group's circle of tolerance and appreciation of differences. This enables group members to feel comfortable enough to participate fully in the discussion.

- **Problem solving:** *Assist* the group in wrestling and dealing with problems — you are not responsible for fixing the problem.

- **Serving as a team player:** In groups that have a recorder or secretary, work with him or her to capture the sense of the discussion. Make sure that the results of the discussion are transferred to the decision-makers.

- **Evaluating:** Ask for feedback from the group to learn how to help the group work more effectively and to ensure that things are going well.

Elements of Clerking a Meeting

Embracing the multi-faceted roles above will enable you to ensure that the consensus process goes well. Your job as facilitator or clerk includes preparation and planning, guiding the group's discussion, and following through to make sure that the necessary people are notified of the summary of the discussion and the group's decision. The following section provides you with guidance and ideas about how to manage each step of the consensus process.

Prepare yourself for the meeting.

As facilitator or clerk, you need to be clear, centered and settled when you clerk a meeting. If you are distracted by personal problems or other matters, you will not be attentive to the needs of the group and to the issues at hand. Before the meeting, it is extremely important for you to take as much time as you need to settle your thoughts and prepare yourself to be a non-anxious presence. Remind yourself of why you were charged with clerking this group. You want to be confident about your abilities to manage the process. You are the model for the kind of atmosphere that will permeate the meeting. If you are harried and distracted, this will affect the group you are clerking.

Get organized.

Before each meeting, you or another person in charge should attend to the following tasks.

- Set the agenda after appropriate consultation with various individuals and groups. Circulate relevant background reports or other materials in advance. Arrange for people to be present at the meeting to present reports and answer questions about them. See Chapter 7 for detailed information about the agenda.

- Set the meeting time and place. Make sure that the meeting space is arranged appropriately; as indicated in Chapter 3, some seating patterns are more conducive to the consensus process. Consult with the person responsible for room set-up or take care of it yourself.

- Arrange for a recorder if the group will make the decision by consensus.

Open the meeting.

As facilitator or clerk, you will want to begin the meeting in such a way that will allow group members to feel comfortable, secure and willing to participate effectively in the discussion and decision-making.

- **Allow for silence:** If appropriate for your group, you can introduce a brief period of silence, explaining that such a pause can help group members step aside from the hectic pace of prior activities and focus on the purpose and goal of the upcoming meeting. Attenders have the opportunity to prepare themselves to search together for unity and for the group's common good.

- **Introduce newcomers and visitors:** Introductions provide a sense of community and hospitality. Newcomers and visitors feel welcomed and current members learn about the new people. You can make the introductions or ask someone else to do this.

- **Explain consensus briefly:** If there are newcomers or if consensus is a new process for the group, you should briefly explain consensus and your role as facilitator or clerk in this process. (See the following page for a sample opening script.)

- **Remind group of its purpose in gathering:** To focus the group even more fully on the reason for gathering you might find it helpful to re-articulate the mission statement of the group and/or identify the reasons underlying the need for a good decision on a given agenda item.

- **Approval of the agenda:** For certain groups, especially small ones, approving the agenda allows the group to feel more ownership of the decision-making process. You can present the whole agenda to the group for its consideration by preparing a typed sheet, a flip chart, or an overhead and then reading through the agenda together. The agenda can include an estimation of time necessary to attend to each item. Keep this brief so that you can begin the discussion.

Present the agenda item and decision context.

At this point you are ready to present the first agenda item. You will return to this point as each new item for discussion is presented.

- Depending on the issue, you can introduce the topic yourself or call on the person who is responsible for the item to provide the group with the information necessary to make the decision.

- Clearly state the issue or concern and what needs to be accomplished. For example: We are charged with making a policy on handicap accessibility to our facilities and programs.

- Indicate the parameters of the group's responsibility. Will the issues identified be handed over to another decision-maker, committee, board or other group? Or will the group make the final decision on a particular issue? Is the group's decision a binding decision for the organization? Are there time or resource constraints for the group's deliberations? Are there other identifiable boundaries or restrictions that may have an impact on choices before the group?

- Allow time for questions of clarification about the content of documents presented in advance. After addressing these questions, you are ready to move into open discussion of the matter.

Don't Know What to Say?

The responsibility of being a facilitator or clerk, especially if you are new at it, can make you nervous, even speechless! In preparing for the meeting, rehearse how you might open the meeting and how you might manage the flow of discussion. To make it easier to start, you may either read the following statement aloud or cover all of the points in your own words, perhaps working from an outline. Sample opening statement to a group using consensus decision-making:

In a consensus process, we operate without making motions. As clerk, I will draw together the threads of the discussion. I will articulate the sense of the agreements we have reached and what remains to be considered. I will verify this with the group and modify this description as we move along in the process.

Today, we are charged with considering the issue of "X" (identify the issue). Our charge is to *(choose one of the following actions)* identify our concerns / make a recommendation / make a decision with regard to this issue.

It is important that we consider the good of the organization and our role in the community as we approach these conversations. We should place these concerns at the center of our efforts.

As the clerk of this session, my role is to remain neutral about the issues and solutions, and about our discussion of them. I will provide guidance to the group only when it seems appropriate to make sure we are following consensus-building practices.

I also would like to suggest some ways you can help this process run smoothly:

- Please speak only when I recognize you.
- Wait until the person speaking has finished before asking for recognition to speak.
- Leave a small amount of silence after the last speaker's words before you speak.
- Please speak to the group as a whole.

I will try to call once on everyone who wants to speak on a given issue before recognizing a request to speak again. We want to make sure everyone has the opportunity to be heard.

We have limited time and many people. Make your point clearly, directly and as briefly as possible. Focus on offering new insights and information. I will try to summarize what I've heard after every four or five speakers, or whenever patterns of thought start to emerge. Please work with me to make sure I have captured the essence of what has been said, especially common threads that are emerging and the differences that still need to be resolved.

Remember that we are looking for the decision that is best for the group as a whole and for our mission as an organization. When we can, we will produce a written statement or minute of our agreements. If we cannot achieve that unity during this meeting, we can develop a clear statement of where we stand in the decision-making process, and we will agree on the next steps we should take to reach consensus.

Is this manner of proceeding acceptable to the group? Does anyone have significant reservations about what I've proposed?

Open and order the discussion.

The job of managing the process now becomes more intense. As facilitator or clerk, you must use all of your senses to pay attention to the group members' body language, eye contact, and verbal cues, which are indicators of how the process is proceeding.

Experienced clerks have differing perspectives on techniques for inviting and ordering input from members, particularly in groups larger than five or six. These approaches include:

- **Stacking:** This is a method for designating the order of speakers as you scan the entire room. You must be sure to remain neutral when determining the order of speakers (Kaner, 1996).

  Formal stacking: Ask participants, "If you plan to speak on this matter, will you please raise your hand (or stand up) so that I may identify you?" Then assign an order to the speakers by gesturing with both palms up (instead of pointing with fingers) or verbally, "John, you'll be first, then Mary, followed by David." As the process continues, other people will ask to be recognized to speak.

  Informal stacking: You do not outwardly indicate the order of speakers, but rather make a mental note of the people who identify themselves, and then call on them one by one. As the process continues, you will need to give an order to speakers when more than one person indicates desire to speak.

  Stacking, however, is not always a good method. It does not always provide a logical sequence for pursuing a particular issue, e.g., the re-marks of the fourth speaker may be more germane to the issues raised by the first speaker than to those of speakers two or three. Group members who feel crowded by the initial array of hands may need more time to ask to be recognized. Stacking may also impede spontaneity, especially in small groups. You may need to encourage the expression of other views. "I recognize that there are other perspectives. May we hear from others who have a different opinion?" "I sense that there is an additional con-cern here. Would someone like to offer something?"

- **Interrupting:** As facilitator or clerk, it is your job to interrupt when neces-sary. You must help create a climate of respect and mutual care in the meet-ing. Someone who rambles on violates this respect. The group expects the facilitator or clerk to interrupt when a speaker has gone on too long, is repetitious, is not addressing the issue at hand, is operating a personal agenda, or is abusive of others (Larrabee, 1993). Even though this may be one of the more difficult tasks, it must be done.

  To ease the awkwardness of interrupting, have some short phrases in mind and prepare to intervene when the speaker takes a breath. The intent is to say "Thank you for what you have said; we have heard your message. Allow me to interrupt you so that others may be heard."

Noted Quaker clerk Art Larrabee states that language that asks for permission is useful. He suggests the following:

"a. May I make a suggestion…?
 b. May I interrupt you…?
 c. Would you be willing for me to…?
 d. May I have your permission to…?" (Larrabee, 1993)

- **Keeping the discussion focused and moving:** If the discussion gets derailed or irrelevant topics are introduced, state, "We began discussing the issue of X but now we are talking about Y. Do we need to note this issue for discussion at a later point and return now to the original topic?" Or you might say: "I think we've gotten off track. Do others agree?" If the group is talking about different but pertinent issues, you should identify the issues, then decide the order in which each one will be discussed.

> **Clerking the Flow of Traffic**
>
> "When I'm in a discussion where the people speak on the heels of each other, I feel like I'm trying to turn left across three lanes of oncoming traffic. Without a long pause, I can't enter the intersection to make my turn. The clerk should provide the left turn signal that slower speakers need."
>
> — Joanna Schofield, Earlham School of Religion and Bethany Theological Seminary

Enhance level and quality of participation.

You can increase the quality of the discussion by maintaining a sense of who is and is not speaking. It may be helpful to use the Group Dynamics Evaluation Form (see Appendix B) to analyze the patterns that develop in a group over time. It is helpful to think through why those patterns may develop. For group members who are seldom heard, is it simply that they are shy in most situations? Some people find it difficult to speak, especially when there is contention or a power differential. Sometimes people do not speak because someone else has stated their ideas and, as good group participants, they do not want to be repetitive. For those who speak frequently and at length or who ramble, you need to determine the content of the individual's remarks. Following are some techniques that can help you address these situations.

- **Listen reflectively and summarize:** As facilitator or clerk, it is important for you to paraphrase what you understand the speaker to have said. Reflecting back may be particularly helpful when a speaker has not spoken succinctly; when there are sensitivities in the group about the lack of power or influence of some members; or when you think the speaker's intent may have been misunderstood by others.

  Some words of caution about reflective listening. This kind of paraphrasing must be done with care so as not to inaccurately interpret, change the meaning of, or judge what has been said. If reflective listening is done for one person, you are almost obligated to do the same for many of the speakers. If you don't, some members may feel left out or perhaps even accuse you of favoritism because you highlighted a particular person's ideas. In the context of open discussion, repeated paraphrasing gets boring and makes group members feel as if they can't understand anything for themselves. It also can slow the pace of the meeting and drain the creative energy out of the group. To avoid this, carefully summarize several speakers' comments together.

- **Ask clarifying questions:** It may be necessary for you to ask a speaker a directive question. "Could you explain more about what you're saying or what you mean?" This technique should be employed to draw out people whose ideas are not yet well formed. By giving a person more time to speak, you are creating an opportunity for that person to develop and organize ideas. Take care to remain neutral; avoid drawing out people simply because they have ideas or opinions that you find interesting.

- **Encourage relevant contributions:** At the outset of the meeting, you can tell the group that members who have not spoken before will be given a chance to speak first. During the meeting, remind the whole group that some members have not spoken yet and then allow time for the less vocal people to speak. By making a mental note of who is and is not speaking, you can talk to them after the meeting, if appropriate. Ask how they thought the meeting went. Ask those who were usually quiet why they did not feel like participating and how you or the group could encourage their participation. Ask the more vocal members what they could do to encourage others to share their views. Periodically, you may want to refer to the Queries for Participants (see Chapter 3) and remind members of their responsibilities.

Synthesize the content of discussion.

While clerking, it is your job to find the common threads of discussion by listening carefully to what people are saying. Let the group know where it is in the process. Periodically, you should synthesize the various strands of thought that arise. Identify areas of common agreement in addition to issues that still need to be resolved and require further discussion. Try out a summary of the agreement as you understand it by drafting a concrete statement and reading it to the group. Sometimes it is appropriate for the recorder to share in the task of synthesizing and drafting. Ask if the group agrees with the synthesis. Be open to suggestions for editing the statement to reflect the central concerns of the group.

If your group is advisory to another decision-maker or group, you and the recorder will be responsible for making sure the synthesis of the discussion is transmitted to the relevant individuals or group. Usually, names and other identifying information of contributors to a discussion or decision are not specified.

A Focus on Decision-Making

In a group that chooses to use consensus to reach a decision, your work as facilitator or clerk becomes more challenging. You now must guide the group in forming its decision with a focus on building the commitment for successful implementation. Remember, however, that your role is to manage the process, not the decision.

Test for agreement.

As the process manager, your task is to move the discussion toward clarity and a decision. When you and the recorder sense that the group is moving toward agreement, ask once again if there are any views, questions or hesitations that have not yet been voiced. Don't rush. Allow time for thought and response.

Summarize the unity that members of the group have reached and express it back to them. Ask for a response. If your formulation doesn't reflect the group's understanding of their unity, you will need to restate it. When testing for agreement, you need to encourage everyone to participate in the decision. You can gauge the comfort of group members by paying attention to the quantity and quality of their participation. Be highly alert to the unspoken as well as to the voiced disagreement with your summary. Again, don't rush the process. You might even want to wait in silence to make sure that people are ready to approve the decision.

> ## I'd Rather Be . . . Pulling Weeds!
>
> "Good clerking allows everyone to leave a meeting (even a long and difficult one) energized to work, and excited about the future. Poor clerking leaves everyone demoralized, tired, and re-examining their commitment to the group and its goals. (It leaves me wondering whether my time wouldn't be better spent gardening.)"
>
> — Ruth Seeley, American Friends Service Committee

Reach a decision.

Once you have formulated a statement of decision, or minute, that captures the group's unity, the recorder notes this statement. Read the minute and ask for the group's approval. Allow time once again for people to consider whether or not they have any remaining concerns before asking for the final approval. Ask the group, "Does the group approve the decision as read?" Wait for the group's verbal response of "Approved." If the response is noticeably cautious in its tone, the clerk may ask group members if they are clearly at unity at this point. If the group is unenthusiastic, ask, "Do I hear your approval?" If the group cannot approve the minute as proposed, unity has not been reached, and the discussion should continue.

The facilitator or clerk and the group must remember that the unity belongs to the group. Sometimes after a decision has been made (especially if the group later discovers that the decision was probably not the best one), a group may point to you as being responsible for making the decision. You are not responsible for this.

In summary, to test for agreement and reach a decision:

- Ask if enough alternatives have been developed and analyzed or if criteria for solving the problem have been met.

- Summarize. Voice the sense of what the group is expressing.

- Propose a statement that reflects the sense of the group. Ask if anyone has unresolved concerns that must be addressed. Pause long enough so that people with concerns have time to collect their thoughts. If people have additional concerns, call for further discussion and revision of the minute until the concerns are resolved.

- Ask for approval of the minute. Remember, no names are noted in the minute because the decision belongs to the group as a whole.

- Read back the written minute of the decision. This is especially crucial for sensitive issues that require agreement on the exact wording of the decision minute.

Clerking Consensus-Building
and Consensus Decision-Making

Use the following brief summary of your role to guide you through clerking the consensus process. Remember, you create the funnel, but not the content. Serve the group rather than promote your personal viewpoint.

Gather necessary resources (information, materials, experts) and circulate (e.g., via e-mail) before the meeting.

Construct the agenda in consultation with individuals, committee, and groups.

Open session and review agenda.

Remind the group to seek a solution that is best for the group. If necessary, do this frequently.

Promote relatively equal opportunities to speak.

Ask questions that help draw out a speaker's meaning. Encourage others to express contrasting views.

Keep group on topic and task, consult with group members about moving the discussion forward.

Call for silent pauses, as needed, to restore the group to its purpose.

Redirect attention to information and ideas that were previously disregarded by the group.

Ask if enough alternatives have been developed, or if criteria for solving the problem have been met.

Express the group feeling or thoughts: identify a conflict, relieve tension, describe group reactions.

Summarize the discussion.

Propose a trial "minute."

Ask for unresolved concerns and pause for responses.

Revise "minute" as necessary.

When concerns have been addressed, ask for approval.

**Announce
approved "minute."**

Handling Difficulties

Conflicts, the styles of participation of certain group members and the availability of time for a decision offer particular challenges even for experienced clerks. Following are some ideas and techniques you might find helpful when handling difficult situations.

Conflicts

As with disagreements, conflicts are part of life. The important thing is to know how to handle them. When conflicts arise, employ one or more of the following:

- Identify the differences and conflicts.

- Encourage expression of missing or conflicting viewpoints, taking care to steer people away from personal attacks or namecalling.

- Redirect attention to information and ideas that were previously disregarded by the group.

- Call for silent pauses as needed to restore the group to its common purpose.

- Enforce open consultation. You may become aware that discussions are occurring outside the meeting that are not supportive of open communication and consensus-building. If so find ways to open those discussions and bring their substance into the group's deliberations.

Too Many Differences, Not Enough Time...in this Meeting

The question of the urgency for a decision requires careful consideration. Is there an external constraint that demands that a decision be reached *today?* If not, will the commitment to that decision and its successful implementation be strengthened by waiting until another meeting can be held? Are the differences so strong that commitment to the group or the relationships within the group may suffer if a decision is pushed at this moment? If a decision is required today, is there a framing of agreement that can permit the group to act now and to iron out other elements of the decision at a later time?

When the group has not reached a decision in the time allotted in this meeting, you should take the following actions:

- Identify issues about which agreement has been reached.

- Identify issues remaining to be resolved.

- Check this understanding with the group and revise if necessary.

- Suggest possible steps for further examination of the issue (e.g., hold the discussion over for the next meeting, define steps to take before the next meeting, or assign the issue to an existing committee or an ad hoc group).

The Difficult Dozen

We all have been in meetings with people who adversely affected the process of the group (or perhaps even you have been the difficult one!). Caroline Estes, an experienced clerk and a founding member of Alpha Farm, an intentional community in western Oregon that uses consensus, provides a list of the *Difficult Dozen* that you as facilitator or clerk are most likely to encounter.

1. **Too talkative:** For the people who go on and on, you can use short questions to interrupt them without being rude. Watch the person as they talk and when they pause to take a breath, ask your question. "Are you nearly finished?" "How much longer will you need?" "Can you summarize your points?" Never interrupt while the person is talking. Another possibility would be to consult with "The Talker" outside of the meeting about how they could limit the length of their contributions. At the beginning of the meeting, establish some parameters about the amount of time allowed for each contribution. To be able to inform the group about how much time is appropriate for each person to speak, divide the number of minutes available for discussion by the number of people in the group. Doing this makes it easier to call attention to the use of time at any point during the meeting.

2. **Shy one:** You need to keep careful track of these people, paying special attention to their body language. If you see them moving forward in their chair, you might simply call on them even though they haven't raised their hand. A simple "Yes?" (not "Do you want to say something?") will often get them speaking before they realize they are doing so. During breaks and before and after meetings, encourage shy and withdrawn people to share their ideas and concerns. Remind them that all pieces of the truth are important, and that the group's decisions are not as complete without their verbal participation. If it is difficult for them to raise their hands, ask if there is some other way (perhaps pulling an ear) that they can signal to you that they are ready to speak.

3. **Whisperer:** The best way to break people of the habit of holding side conversations is while it is happening. Stop the meeting and ask "Do you have something to share on the subject at hand?" This must be done in such a way that is short of embarrassing, but sharp enough to get the point across.

4. **Repeater:** Usually you can manage the people who tend to repeat things by incorporating their first contribution into a summary. This gives them a sense of being heard. Another option would be to have a scribe write contributions on a board or flip chart. Once the repeaters see their comments in writing, they usually do not feel the need to repeat.

5. **Angry person:** Anger appears in many forms and for many reasons. If there is a heated argument between two people, you as facilitator or clerk need to physically step between them to cut the negative energy. If someone's anger about a certain issue is blocking progress, ask the person, "If the concern you have raised is noted in the minute, will that satisfy you?" When you sense that a person's anger has disrupted the group's ability to work, ask the group, "Do we need to take a short break?" It would not be wise to simply ask, "What should we do?" You need to be directive by providing a set of options or simply making the decision to call a recess.

6. **Constant objector:** Usually an objector is someone who needs attention. To provide that attention in a positive manner, assign a scribe to write down all of the

objections presented. This does the twofold job of honoring the person who has raised the objection and compels the group to wrestle with these issues. As the discussion continues, point out when items on that list have been addressed and resolved. There are times when objections are helpful and times when they are not. When objections are raised during a brainstorming session, you as facilitator or clerk should acknowledge them and then ask the objector to wait to bring them up again during the discussion when the objections can be addressed.

7. **Devil's advocate:** Other group members often consider a "devil's advocate" to be problematic, but in fact a constructive devil's advocate can play a very helpful role. Timing the contributions of a devil's advocate is important; their evaluative remarks are not helpful during brainstorming but can be most useful in assessing alternatives. By pointing out reasons why an idea won't work, a devil's advocate provides the group an opportunity to address defects in a proposal. A devil's advocate can also voice a concern or perspective that has not been voiced by members of the group but is important to consider. You should thank the devil's advocates directly for their contributions. Once devil's advocates are taken seriously, they usually feel that their role has been completed.

8. **Authoritarian:** When people use such language as "It's well known that ...," they are claiming generalized authority for their opinions. You should ask them for the source. Other people might try to speak for the whole group by saying, "We all ..." or "Everybody thinks..." Ask them to please use first-person or "I" statements. The authoritarian claims authority for a particular position. In contrast, the devil's advocate raises questions but does not claim authority for an alternative perspective.

9. **Opinionated member:** These people do not pose much of a problem if their contributions are brief. If people frequently offer lengthy opinions, speak with them outside of the meeting. Remind them that the simple phrase "That friend speaks my mind" or use of clear body language (such as nodding their heads) is a more concise way of offering their opinion.

10. **General - admiral - dictator:** These people consider themselves to be the "real" leader of the group because they feel as if they could do a better job at managing the meeting than the facilitator or clerk. You *must* be willing to stand up to people who constantly say "I know..." or "We need to..." One option would be not to recognize them to speak, but most groups are in the habit of acquiescing to them. You could also remind them that once they offer their insight or idea they must not try to maintain ownership of it.

11. **Manipulator:** A lighthearted way to handle a manipulator is to say at the beginning of the meeting, "Will everyone who has a hidden agenda please put it on the table." Then when someone begins to manipulate the discussion, you or other group members can refer back to the opening statement and say, "Oops, I see your agenda."

12. **Agenda hostage-taker:** These individuals feel that their items are more important than anything else on the agenda and so will try to prevent the process from moving forward. You must be very firm in limiting their stall tactics. Some possible responses might be: "In courtesy to the group and to the remaining agenda items, we must hold to the time limits"; "We are moving on to the next item"; "We will return to this item"; or "We will put this item on the list for the agenda maker to bring forward next time."

- Ask for consent to move forward in this way.
- In rare instances, you may need to direct the proceedings or make decisions on behalf of the group. This may occur when there is enduring conflict *and* a member cannot unite with the group in moving forward nor offer a viable alternative after respectful consideration by the group.

Evaluate Group Process

Periodic evaluation of how the group is working together will allow members to reflect on their level of participation and commitment to the process. An evaluation also will provide you with specific information about how you are managing the process. It is often helpful to have someone observe how group members work together during the consensus process and give feedback to the group. The Consensus Practices Checklist (Appendix A) and Group Dynamics Evaluation Form (Appendix B) are two tools for doing this.

Chapter 7
Agenda

Introduction

The agenda is the "road map" that guides the group through the various issues that must be addressed. This chapter supplies groups with recommendations for careful preparation, consideration, approval, and modification of the agenda. The last section will be useful for facilitators or clerks as they work with others in creating the agenda.

Sources for Agenda Items

Careful preparation of the agenda is critical to the success of the meeting. The facilitator or clerk and the recorder collaborate on this task. Items for the agenda usually arise from the following three sources:

- Items held over from previous meetings. The facilitator or clerk and the recorder should review minutes from previous meetings to remind themselves which issues need to be brought forward.

- New items of business. These should be submitted by a deadline established by the facilitator or clerk.

- Reports from established standing committees, ad hoc committees, work groups, task forces, etc.

Submitting Items for the Agenda

To enable careful preparation of the agenda, the sponsor of an agenda item should provide the facilitator or clerk with the following:

- Background information, which will help the facilitator or clerk determine an item's priority level.

- If needed, handouts to be circulated to all members.

- An estimate of the time that will be required to discuss the item at the meeting.

- The level of consideration the item requires. Such levels include:
  a. Information to be reported to the group.
  b. Introduction of an issue that will take considerable work.
  c. Brainstorming so that input can be taken back to a committee or work group.
  d. Discussion of something the group will make a decision about at a subsequent meeting.
  e. Items requiring a decision.

During the meeting, the sponsor of the item provides introductory information and answers questions. If a committee or work group brings an item to the agenda, one person is identified to provide the introduction and to direct questions to other group members during the meeting.

An agenda submission form is sometimes used; see example on the next page. This can be altered easily to reflect any organizational structure.

Reviewing the Agenda and Documents in Advance

Agendas include some or all of the following:

- The topic, level of consideration, time allotted, and sponsor for each item on the agenda.

- A list of any items that were proposed but not placed on the agenda.

Group members should have the opportunity to review the agenda, either ahead of time (circulate it by e-mail or other means of effective communication with the group) or at the beginning of the meeting. Sending the agenda out along with written reports and materials pertinent to the discussion before the meeting informs members what issues will be discussed at the meeting and allows them time to reflect on their views and think of ideas and possible solutions. Sponsors of agenda items can send the materials directly or they can be sent by the clerk along with the agenda.

Approval of the Agenda

In some organizations, the agenda is set by the chairperson. In other groups, it is advisable for the facilitator or clerk to ask for approval of the draft agenda at the beginning of the meeting. Groups vary as to how precisely they prepare their agendas and how stringently they stick to time limits associated with the discussion of various agenda items.

During the meeting, the agenda should be clearly accessible to everyone in the group, either in printed copies distributed to everyone or printed in large letters on a flip chart or a board. Either the sponsor of an item or the facilitator or clerk can make sure that copies of written reports and materials are also available at the meeting.

Agenda Item Submission Form

From: _____

For meeting on: _____ Date Submitted: _____

Please check one of the following to indicate what meeting
should consider this item:

___ Whole membership   ___ Executive group
___ Board of Trustees   ___ Administrative or Department Group
___ Ad hoc group (specify):   ___ Committee (specify):

___ Other (specify): _____

___ Item/problem description: _____

_____

_____

Nature of consideration desired:

___ Information/report   ___ Introduction
___ Brainstorm   ___ Discussion

___ Decision (please specify if there is a deadline)_____

Handouts to be provided to the group:

_____

_____

Estimated time this agenda item will require:

_____

NOTE: If the discussion of this agenda item is not completed
at the meeting, it will need to be resubmitted.

For agenda coordinator's use only.

Kind of consideration this should be given: _____

_____

Estimated time it will take: _____

Priority relative to other items submitted for the agenda: _____

_____

**If this form has been returned to you, further clarification is needed.
Please resubmit with more information about the items circled above.**

Before approving the agenda, allow time for members to ask questions of clarification and to make modifications to the agenda. Such changes may include:

- Moving an item from the "proposed" list onto the active agenda.

- Modifying the amount of time planned for particular items. Sometimes this occurs after an item's sponsor explains why an agenda item needs more time than has been allowed in the draft agenda, and the group agrees after placing the sponsor's request in the context of the full range of business that must be accomplished at the meeting. Many groups operate under the assumption that a proposed agenda will be accepted with few alterations. By approving the agenda, group members authorize the facilitator or clerk to hold them to the topics and time limits as listed.

Modifying the Agenda During a Meeting

During the course of a meeting, the group may choose to modify the agenda to:

- Add an item that has come up in the course of discussion.

- Change the level of discussion on an item.

- Change the amount of time devoted to an item.

The facilitator or clerk helps the group make the agenda change explicit.

A change in the agenda also may be made less formally. For example, the facilitator or clerk can say, "This topic is taking longer than anticipated, but we are making headway. Can we agree to spend an extra 15 minutes on X, and take that time away from the discussion of Y?"

In the absence of a deliberate change of agenda, discussion should be focused on the item under consideration. Tangents are appropriate only when they help illuminate the topic that is being discussed.

Guidance for the Facilitator or Clerk in Setting Agendas

Before the Meeting

Answering the following questions will help the facilitator or clerk specify which issues should be addressed and in what order:

- How do the issues to be discussed fit into the overall goals of the group? If the group is part of a larger institution, how do the issues align with the institutional goals?

- How difficult will it be for the group to reach a decision on this issue?

- How much meeting time will probably be needed to discuss and resolve this issue?

- What are the time constraints within which a decision must be made?

- Should this issue be addressed by the whole group or should it be handed over to a sub-group or committee?

- If it is a complicated item, would it be more prudent to break it into several issues to be discussed one at a time?

- If necessary, could this issue be postponed until the next meeting?

The order in which items are discussed is critical to the outcome of the meeting. Put items in an order that will help create energy. The first agenda item should be one that can be resolved without difficulty. Experiencing a sense of accomplishment energizes the group to be able to deal with more difficult issues. Alternate between difficult issues and the easier or more routine issues (for example, committee reports) to allow the group to rest and gather strength. If several issues are difficult, it might be necessary to take a break at a strategic point in the meeting.

Try to imagine how the meeting might flow. Sometimes the facilitator or clerk will estimate time allotments inaccurately; the item that seemed would only take five minutes to resolve may in fact take much longer. With practice, however, the facilitator or clerk will begin to recognize how to anticipate and manage the normal ebbs and flows of discussion.

During the agenda-making process, the facilitator or clerk needs to talk with the stakeholders in each issue to understand their needs and concerns about the possible outcomes better. A stakeholder may be the person who will be affected by the decision, or it may be the person or group who has the power to make the final decision and/or implement it. If the stakeholders cannot be present at the meeting, they should help arrange for someone to attend who can voice their interests and concerns; otherwise, problems are likely to arise when the decision is implemented.

The facilitator or clerk also should consult with the people or groups who are sponsoring a particular agenda item to clarify and understand the issue. Sponsors should be reminded that it is not their job to make the decision; their task is to educate group members about options and inform them how the committee arrived at its recommendations.

During the Meeting

The facilitator's or clerk's role as manager of the process begins with reviewing and modifying the agenda. Take care not to let a sizeable portion of the meeting time be taken up with this first step.

If the meeting time is running out and agenda items still have not been considered, ask the group, "It doesn't look as if we will get through all of the agenda today. What do you suggest we do?" Ask them if they would like to stay to continue to work on remaining issues or if they would like to meet at another time to finish.

Chapter 8
Making and Taking Minutes

Introduction

In consensus decision-making, the word "minute" is used to describe two types of written records. The minutes of a meeting are just like those of most boards of directors and other governing bodies: they summarize discussions and state decisions made by the group. The other use of the word "minute" in consensus decision-making, however, is not so common: it refers to a minute, or written record, of a specific decision that has been reached through consensus.

The person who takes the minutes is called the recording clerk or the recorder. This role may be somewhat different from the secretary in other groups; like the clerk or facilitator, the recorder is neutral about issues, and he or she may actively work with the clerk during the meeting to formulate a given minute.

The Minutes of the Meeting

When done well, meeting minutes have the following characteristics:

- Every item on the agenda gets an entry in the minutes.

- Entries about items presented for reasons other than making a specific decision (e.g., for information, introduction, brainstorming, or discussion) should summarize the discussion. The summary should present only the salient points, covering the main thrust of the discussion, the concerns that have been raised, and ways that were formulated to carry the discussion along.

- Names associated with particular ideas, statements or positions are seldom included in the minutes of a meeting. Once offered, ideas are considered the property of the group, and the whole group is responsible for the decisions that are made. A name might be mentioned when someone makes a presentation on behalf of a committee, agrees to do a specific task for the group, such as researching an issue, or when that person must be contacted to begin implementing a decision. When names are included, proper legal names (not nicknames) are used.

- Decisions are also recorded in the minutes, as outlined below.

- Generally both the facilitator or clerk and the recorder sign the minutes since they both were involved in producing them.

Consensus Process

This is a model of the consensus-building and decision-making process that occurs in a meeting. The circle with F/C represents the facilitator or clerk.

Stage 1

At the beginning of the meeting, group members hold different viewpoints on the matter in discussion.

Stage 2

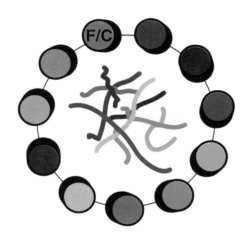

Members share information, questions, alternative solutions and concerns. Positions are not attached to the people who offer them. The facilitator or clerk coordinates the process and periodically summarizes the discussion.

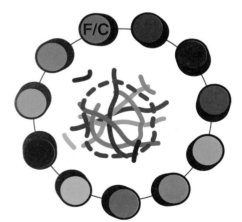

Stage 3

A pattern based on the discussion begins to appear.

Stage 4

The facilitator or clerk proposes a statement of the pattern of agreement. When group members believe that the statement accurately reflects their decision, they approve it as a minute of consensus. Note that some ideas and threads of the discussion have fallen by the wayside.

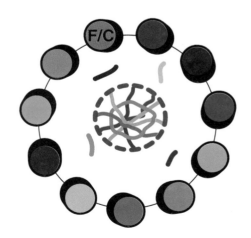

Conflict in Consensus

At times there is an issue that evokes a great deal of conflict. It is important for members to voice their concerns so that real consensus can be reached. Engaging conflict can lead to creative solutions — solutions that often astonish even the skeptics. For more information about conflict, see Chapter 5: When We Disagree and Chapter 9: Dissent.

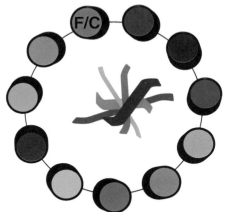

Stage 1

Group members share information that reflects their different perspectives.

Stage 2

Facilitator or clerk (F/C) summarizes the convergence and differences in the discussion. Even though active listening and discussion continues, possibly over several meetings, members still do not share a strong, common, coherent solution.

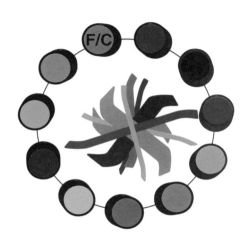

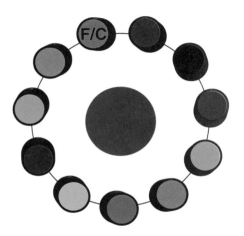

Stage 3

A member suggests a "purple" idea. After careful consideration, the appropriateness of this idea becomes clear to the other group members.

Stage 4

The facilitator or clerk states that the sense of the group is purple. There is no further dissent, and the "purple" solution is approved.

The Minute of Decision

When the group is nearing agreement on a decision, the facilitator or clerk will formulate a tentative statement of the agreement, or "minute of decision." The recorder writes it down and reads it back to the group for approval or response.

The minute may be approved as read, or discussed further. Points raised in the discussion may lead to alterations in the wording. After each revision, the recorder reads the altered minute back to the group for its approval or further discussion.

It is vital that everyone participating in the decision is able to hear, understand and agree to the specific wording of any minute of decision that is recorded.

Example of Minutes and Minutes of Decision

The Building Committee met at 7:00 p.m. on July 14, 1999, at the office on 309 South Oak. All of the members were in attendance. The clerk presented the issue: do we want to make an offer to purchase the property at 2001 S. Magnolia for our new offices? Another organization has made a bid on it and we must decide today if we want to make a counter-offer.

Concerns were raised about the appropriateness of this property for our long-term growth; the costs of renovation for handicap access and of long-term upkeep; availability of financing; and uncertainty about re-zoning to permit our proposed use. The most serious concern was our current internal organization for arranging financing, obtaining a zoning variance and planning for renovations in the limited time available. After careful consideration, including a moment of silence, we reached the following agreements:

Minute 1: A financing subcommittee will be formed to raise the necessary funds. Pedro Ramirez, Tanya Williams and Ann Jones will serve on this committee for the next year.

Minute 2: With greater clarity about our internal organization, we will offer the attached contract to purchase the property at 2001 South Magnolia.

Respectfully submitted,
Rebecca Marshall, Clerk
Jim Moore, Recorder

Since the decision is made by the group as a whole and all are responsible for it, no names are used in the minute of decision — unless an individual who disagrees with the decision asks to have his or her opposition recorded.

Noting Minutes of Decision

When a minute of decision is noted in the minutes of the meeting, it should be numbered and written in the exact wording the group has approved. The meeting minutes should also include a paragraph summarizing the issue or problem the minute was intended to address, the process by which the decision was reached, and relevant concerns that were discussed.

The meeting minutes should include a specific statement of how the group will implement the decision called for in the minute. To the extent that it is possible, the recorder should include the names of people who will follow through and a timetable for action.

Minutes of decision become the official binding record of the decisions of the group. Each decision can only be changed by a new consensus.

The Minute of Process

When an issue is not completely resolved or the discussion is not completed, the recording clerk should write down what issues have been resolved and how, what issues remain to be discussed, and what is the proposed process for continuing the discussion. The concerns should be listed because it helps the committee or group to take responsibility for the process and to understand more explicitly what needs additional work.

The Recorder

The recorder works in collaboration with the facilitator or clerk to provide accurate written records of what occurs in a meeting. The recorder can provide invaluable assistance to the facilitator or clerk by paying attention to the verbal and visual indicators of what is going on in the meeting. The facilitator or clerk has the responsibility of verbally synthesizing the agreement the group has reached. It is the recorder's job to express the agreement in written form. Like the facilitator or clerk, the recorder does not participate in the discussion and is neutral about the content. The recorder also does not editorialize or add personal views to the minutes.

The Tasks of the Recorder

- Write the minutes of a meeting, including summaries of the discussion about each agenda item; a brief description of the intent of each minute of decision; and the exact wording of minutes of decision as approved in the meeting.

- Report matters factually and simply. Keep in mind that minutes of a meeting become historical documents. Include sufficient information and details of the discussion and decisions so that people who read the minutes at a later date will be able to understand the content of the concerns underlying a particular decision.

- Help the facilitator or clerk formulate the wording of minutes of decision during the meeting.

- Present the minutes of the previous meeting. This is done in a pre-arranged format in which the group is invited to offer corrections. Sometimes the minutes are mailed out, sent by e-mail or posted in a pre-designated place to give people time to review them before the meeting. In other instances, the minutes are read aloud at the beginning of the current meeting, or time is allowed for people to read them.

- Correct the minutes according to changes agreed upon when the minutes are approved.

- Keep copies of the approved minutes of all meetings, bound in some fashion and formatted for readability. This duty is assigned to someone else. This binder preserves both the short- and long-term memory of the group.

Attributes of a Good Recorder

The following are some characteristics to look for when selecting a recorder:

- Ability to attend meetings regularly and promptly, and to complete work in a timely manner.

- Ability to listen, summarize and record accurately.

- Ability to remain neutral, not adding personal ideas to the minutes.

- Skill in succinctly stating ideas.

- Skill in producing good, readable documents.

Chapter 9
When Disagreement Deepens

Introduction

Ways of engaging differences in consensus-building were discussed in Chapter 4. But sometimes differences and disagreements can deepen into dissent. When a group is using consensus decision-making to reach a final decision, persistent differences may pose a special challenge. In some forms of consensus, the decision rules permit an individual to block the group from moving forward because of a personal preference for another alternative. These approaches are largely based on individual rights.

The form of consensus presented in this book approaches dissent differently than other forms of consensus do. All members of a group are expected to consider the good of the group, the insight of the individual, and the importance of ongoing relationships. The individual and the group are held in tension because both the individual's insight and the group's wisdom are important. (For more background on how Quakers approach this issue, see Chapter 11). As a consensus decision-making group faces persistent differences and dissent, dissenters and other members of the group should engage one another respectfully.

What Group Members Should Do

Group members may find themselves moving toward agreement, and yet they are concerned about the views of one or more group members who have expressed strong dissent. When this happens, reflecting on the following questions can be helpful for those who wish to be sure they have carefully considered dissenting viewpoints:

- Has the group given the dissenter ample opportunity to explain his/her concerns about the direction in which the group is moving?

- Has the group made an earnest effort to consider the dissenter's concerns?

- Is the group clear about what the dissenter has been saying? If not, is there a way for the group to gain greater clarity about the dissenter's concerns?

- Has the group ignored or overlooked, perhaps due to misunderstanding or to the urgency to make a decision, any valid concerns raised by the dissenter?

- Has the group considered obtaining crucial information regarding concerns raised by the dissenter before making a decision?

What Dissenting Members Should Do

Sometimes, one or more members of the group find themselves unable to resolve their concerns and ideas about an issue. They may be strongly convinced that a particular course of action goes against the best interests of the group. When this happens, the following questions can help them become clearer about their concerns, why they have them, and what can be done to address their concerns:

- Is the good of the group the central focus of my concerns about this issue?

- Have I made an earnest effort to understand the matter by attending meetings at which it has been discussed, studying the issue with the group, and being available for discussion?

- Have I listened to others and made an effort to understand their views?

- Have I expressed my concerns clearly? If not, is there a better way to state them?

- Have I considered alternate solutions? If not, what alternatives might I suggest?

- If I cannot propose an alternate solution, how would I feel if the group moved in the proposed direction? Could I live with that decision in the interest of the group, even though it is not my preference?

- Am I in partial disagreement with the group? If so, does it seem better for the group to take this action now than to take none? If so, should I remain silent as the decision is approved or should I state that I withdraw my concern?

- If I am willing to let the decision stand even though I do not agree with it, should I state my disagreement and then say I'll stand aside? Should I ask that my disagreement and my decision to stand aside be recorded in the minutes?

- Do I feel that no decision would be better for the group than this one? Can I clearly state why I am in such disagreement and cannot unite with the decision?

If Dissent Persists

If, after weighing the above considerations, the dissenter still has concerns that stand in the way of agreeing with the group's decision, this form of consensus practice provides the following options:

Stand aside

The dissenter steps out of the decision-making process and permits the decision to be made. The dissenter intends to abide by the decision. Sometimes, the dissenter asks that his/her concerns be recorded in the minutes.

Withdraw concern

The dissenter can withdraw his/her concern if s/he believes that it is better for the group to take this action than to take none at this time.

Unable to unite

The dissenter states that s/he cannot support the decision, and why. In taking this position, the dissenter hopes to persuade the group to keep searching for a solution that addresses concerns that s/he believes are in the interest of the group as a whole.

For its part, the group then decides whether to set the matter aside until a later time, have further discussion, or continue moving toward a decision.

The Facilitator's or Clerk's Role

When a dissenter continues to state inability to unite with the decision, even after the processes for dealing with differences noted in Chapter 4 have been employed, the facilitator or clerk must decide whether the dissent warrants further consideration. The decision about whether to discuss the matter further may be based on whether the group can delay making a decision, whether the dissenter has raised concerns that the group should address, and whether the dissenter is acting in the interest of the group and its values, mission and guiding philosophy. The facilitator or clerk then has the following options:

Continue discussion

If the group feels it would be best to resolve the concerns of the dissenter(s) before moving forward with a decision, discussion can continue if time permits. At any point, the group can decide to end the discussion and proceed with the decision, or to lay down the matter.

Proceed with decision

If the dissenting member stands aside or is deemed not to be acting in the interests of the group, the facilitator or clerk may propose a minute of decision and ask for its approval by the group. The concerns of the dissenting member should be recorded in the minutes of the meeting.

Lay down the matter

If the group is divided over a decision or does not feel ready to make a decision, the matter can be laid down for the time being, if time permits. A date should be set for considering whether the matter should come before the group again at that time.

Dealing with Dissent

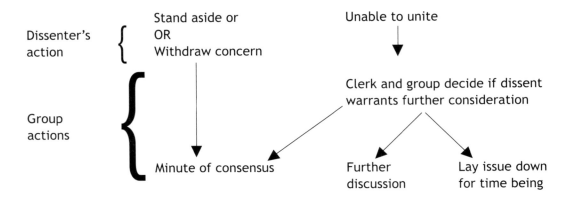

If a minute of decision is approved and dissent continues, the decision still stands. If the group determines that an earlier decision requires modification, the consensus process begins anew so that the group may make a new decision.

Chapter 10
Consensus and
Other Decision-Making Approaches

Introduction

Groups and organizations that use consensus decision-making may combine this process with other approaches. Different issues may be handled through different processes. This chapter briefly explores several approaches to decision-making: consensus decision-making, hierarchical decision-making with and without consensus-building, parliamentary procedure with majority rule, and parliamentary procedure with consensus-building. This information will be helpful as you consider if and when consensus decision-making will work for your group.

Choosing which decision-making processes to use in a given situation depends on various factors, including:

- The information available in the group and the likelihood that it will be shared under various processes.

- The importance of having broad-based support for the decision.

- The willingness to engage conflict during the process.

- The level of cooperation and trust that already exists among members of a work group or that needs to be developed for future decision-making or implementation.

- The amount of time available to the group to make a decision, considered in relation to the amount of time required for implementation if conflict is ongoing.

- Importance of satisfaction of decision-makers and their expectations about inclusion and voice.

In exploring the contexts in which different forms or combinations of decision-making are effective, we draw from both our own experience and the literature on situational leadership and participation, particularly Vroom and Jago (1988). For those who are familiar with situational leadership literature the format of this chapter will seem familiar. For those who are not, each type of decision-making is appropriate under different combinations of conditions.

Consensus Decision-Making

Consensus decision-making is a very old form of democracy used in a variety of cultures (Mansbridge, 1980). As indicated earlier, the approach to consensus presented in this book is based on the particular form of corporate decision-making used by the Religious Society of Friends for more than 350 years. This approach serves groups well in situations in which ongoing relationships are important and adversarial decisions will have a continuing negative impact on the performance of the group. Experience has shown that people are much more likely to change their behavior for the good of the group if they fully understand, through discussion, why the change is needed and if they have a voice in shaping the changes. The consensus decision-making process, then, creates a shared sense of the group's responsibility for the outcome.

> "Quaker-based consensus is not just a tool — it's a way of life," says Bill Remmes, Rural Health Group Inc.

Consensus decision-making is useful in hierarchical groups that have a person-in-charge and in groups that may not have a single authority based on position, such as boards or self-led teams. Situations in either type of group in which consensus decision-making may be appropriate are:

- When sharing information and seeking common ground in deciding what to do will save time in implementing the proposed solution.

- When a minority voice might suggest important concerns or stimulate innovative ideas.

- When conflict can be acknowledged and used constructively.

- When it is important to develop the group's capacity to work together over the longer term.

Voting to Use Consensus

The new president of a small-city Chamber of Commerce introduced consensus to his board of directors as an alternative means of making decisions. The board voted to use consensus on a trial basis. At the end of this period, board members agreed that the experience had been so positive that they wanted to continue using the consensus process.

When these conditions have been met, there are some other conditions that may suggest the use of consensus decision-making. In a group that has used parliamentary procedure with majority rule, consensus decision-making will be particularly useful when coalitional behavior that can result from voting and majority rule is likely to undermine commitment to the group and its work in the future. In a hierarchical group or organization, the following considerations may influence a manager to use consensus decision-making for resolving a particular issue:

Situation 1: The work group must have a high commitment to the solution for it to be successfully implemented, and group members are unlikely to have sufficient commitment if the person in charge makes the decision.

Situation 2: Members of the group have sufficient information and expertise to make a good decision, and they support the organizational goals to be attained in solving the problem.

Situation 3: There is conflict within the group about what solution is best, and group members are unlikely to commit to a solution if the person in charge makes the decision. (Adapted from Vroom and Jago, 1988).

Introducing Decisions by Consensus

If your group is accustomed to using other methods of decision-making, you could decide to use consensus only for certain decisions or particular types of decisions. It is best to use consensus for those decisions that require broad-based commitment for their implementation; for example, setting fund-raising goals in a nonprofit organization or sales goals in a business.

Executives in charge can introduce consensus in a group for resolving particular issues. It doesn't necessarily require giving up executive prerogative to define boundaries for seeking solutions. An executive can also remind the group of policy constraints that make a particular idea infeasible at a given time. It does help to have a member of the group besides the person in charge serve as the facilitator or clerk. Even if the boss is present, members tend to speak more freely when someone else is in charge of the process.

Potential Drawbacks of Consensus Decision-Making

In a hierarchical setting, consensus decision-making requires people who traditionally may have had responsibility for making decisions to relinquish that responsibility to the group, and there may be reasons why that does not seem appropriate to them. In situations in which voting and parliamentary process have been favored, group members may be concerned that conflicts cannot be successfully resolved by consensus and that a decision may not be reached.

Measuring Time

When deciding what decision-making process to use, consider the total time needed to make AND implement the decision — don't just focus on the amount of meeting time used to reach a decision.

It often takes longer to make decisions using consensus decision-making. This is especially true when the process is new to a group. As a result, some groups would rather continue to accept decisions that satisfy a majority of their members than to invest time in learning how to use a new process or in working through differing viewpoints to find a solution which every group member can support.

Making the effort to build consensus, however, usually reduces the time required to implement a decision. Time spent building consensus can reduce the delays in effective implementation that result from not taking into account the concerns of some members.

Hierarchical Decision-Making

In some situations it is appropriate for a person in charge to make top-down decisions. In a life-or-death emergency with limited time for response, to use an extreme example, it is obviously far better to rely on the rapid-fire instructions of trained emergency personnel than to convene a meeting to deliberate about how to proceed. Top-down decisions are appropriate in other situations as well.

The following situations illustrate the kinds of factors that are relevant when choosing to make top-down decisions:

> **Situation 1:** The person in charge has the relevant experience, information and expertise to identify alternatives and make the choice; the group members will accept the decision of the person in charge; and making a decision quickly is more important than developing the capacity of the group members to take more responsibility for decisions themselves.

> **Situation 2:** The quality of the decision is not important because any one of several alternatives could solve the problem, and commitment of the group members is not important to successful implementation. (Adapted from Vroom and Jago, 1988).

Potential Drawbacks of Top-Down Decision-Making

We probably can think of times when plans handed down by the boss are not successfully implemented. Sometimes those with position power are unaware that their employees have relevant information and experience or that it is difficult for them to volunteer their concerns to the "boss." Sometimes the plan fails because the group feels that there are problems with it, but members have little or no opportunity to suggest changes, so they are never truly committed to making the plan work. Sometimes group members are aware of key factors that would influence implementation but undervalue their input by not mentioning this to the boss.

Consensus-Building Combined with Hierarchical Decision-Making

Consensus-building practices can be combined with hierarchical decision-making, providing a method to guide consultation even when a supervisor or executive is the only one in a position to determine the final decision. In these situations, it is very important that the decision-maker clarifies at the beginning of the process that the group is acting in an advisory capacity only and that the reasons for the final decision be given in terms that explicitly address the group's recommendation.

Consultative decision-making in a group that uses consensus-building processes may be appropriate when a high-quality decision is important and commitment of those involved is necessary for successful implementation. This is especially true when these factors are combined with the following conditions:

> **Situation 1:** Development of group capacity is important, and the relevant group or organizational members have common organizational goals but have conflict over preferred solutions.

Situation 2: High commitment is not likely without involvement of others in making the decision.

Situation 3: The person in charge doesn't have the necessary information for a high-quality decision without input from several subordinates, and either the group has agreement on organizational goals or the alternatives and criteria for solving them are known. (Adapted from Vroom and Jago, 1988)

In these situations, having a facilitator or clerk (someone other than the executive or the person in charge) guide the discussion often generates more openness in identifying options. Group members feel more free to express their concerns about possible courses of action when there is a facilitator or clerk — even if the boss is present in the room.

Parliamentary Procedure and Majority Rule

Business Uses Consensus . . . Up to a Point!

The president of an international distributor of computer memory products writes:

"I formed a board of directors for my company out of individuals both within and outside of the company. All decisions made by my board are made using the consensus process that I learned at a workshop. Decision-making is much slower than under our old system, but because everybody is personally ego-involved with every decision, we don't seem to be making very many mistakes. Corporate revenues have grown almost 30% and profits are up over 50% since last July when I changed the decision-making procedures.

"Consensus decision-making only seems to work in the corporate environment up to a point. An impasse will occasionally arise in a situation that demands immediate resolution. Rather than playing the game of waiting to see who will stand aside first, I have removed the discussion from the table, and made the decision myself. This is a somewhat dangerous way to break the rules, but ultimately, this is my company. I will take responsibility for my own mistakes."

- Aaron Buckley, President of Ramjet, Inc.

In the contemporary Western world, we often think of parliamentary procedure — a fairly new form of democratic decision-making in human history (Mansbridge, 1980) — as the primary way of making choices in democracy. We often use parliamentary procedure and majority rule for deciding what to do in national and local governance and in the boards of community and business organizations. *Robert's Rules of Order* is used to guide decision-making in many organizations.

When Parliamentary Procedure with Majority Rule Is Most Useful

This approach is most useful when the following conditions exist:

- The group understands that the need for a quick decision is more pressing than sharing information.

- Clear alternatives are identified and further discussion would not likely result in innovative ideas.

- The group is willing to accept majority rule when a common solution cannot be found.

- Group members believe that their differences are so great that they cannot find common ground or a unifying interest among themselves.

- Neither successful implementation of decisions nor the legitimacy of the group's future actions will be undermined by a minority group.

Potential Drawbacks of Majority Rule

We all probably know of situations in which plans adopted through majority rule fail. Sometimes, decision-making by majority rule becomes a combative or fragmented debate and minority viewpoints are silenced (Gastil, 1993). Minority members may show low commitment to the task and perform more poorly when they are required to implement the decision without further input (Hunton, Price and Hall, 1996). Sometimes majority rule fails because the members of the losing side turn their energy toward sabotage or plotting to win the next vote. Or it fails because the plan that is adopted through voting cannot be successfully implemented without broader support than the majority alone can provide.

Community in Unity

Three state land-grant universities and community stakeholders formed a new group, Steering Committee of Visions for Change: Communities Working Together to Strengthen Food and Fiber Systems, to rethink the vision, mission and relationship of these important institutions to diverse communities and their constituencies. The members of the Steering Committee decided they needed a new way of making decisions as well as a new mission. They combined clerking with a chairperson role and consensus-building with a vote once consensus was reached. The co-clerks of this committee were a Native American from a community organization and a white farmer. According to the assistant director, the strength of this approach is that the voices of community stakeholders that were not heard or were easily marginalized in a majority rule setting are now being heard.

Parliamentary Procedure with Consensus-Building

Although the two processes differ in how final decisions are made, consensus-building processes can be used in combination with *Robert's Rules of Order* and voting. Rather than being an adversarial process, discussion can be conducted as a learning process with the intent of reaching clear understanding of the concerns of group members. A group can adopt norms that prohibit calling for a vote until there is a consensus on the issue. The chairperson's role can be structured as clerk-chair, giving emphasis to the identification of the aspects of the issue on which the group agrees and of the differences and concerns that still need to be resolved.

This combined approach may be considered when:

- It is important to engage marginalized subgroups in sharing information and broad-based support is important to support implementation and legitimacy of the decision.

- Cooperation and trust need to be built.

- Time to make the decision is less important than the time to implement with support of subgroups.

- Legal constraints require a vote to be recorded.

A Comparison: *Robert's Rules of Order* and Consensus

Robert's Rules of Order with Majority Vote	Consensus Decision-Making
A single motion can constrain the discussion.	Multiple concerns and information are shared until the sense of the group is clear.
Discussion takes the form of a debate with a win-lose approach.	Discussion involves active listening and sharing information.
Few constraints are placed on the order or frequency of speaking.	Norms limit number of times one asks to speak to ensure that each speaker is fully heard.
Ideas are treated as the property of the speaker; motions are noted with names.	Ideas and solutions belong to the group; no names are recorded.
Differences are resolved by voting on a motion.	Differences resolved by discussion. Clerk identifies areas of agreement and names disagreements to push discussion deeper.
Chair calls for a vote.	Facilitator or clerk articulates the sense of the discussion, asks if there are other concerns, and proposes a "minute" of the decision.
Winners and losers are identified. Decision belongs to the winners.	Group as a whole is responsible for the decision, and the decision belongs to the group.
Chair's vote can determine the decision when votes are tied.	Facilitator or clerk can discern if a person who is not uniting with the decision is acting without concern for the group or in selfish interest.
Minority perspectives suppressed in majority vote.	Dissenters' perspectives are embraced.

A Caution on Combining Approaches

Some people judge the form of decision-making that their institution practices as nothing more than majority rule with an overlay of discussion. Majority rule in this form squelches the minority voice while the "winners" leave the business meeting with a smug sense of having included all opinions in the decision.

Tom Kirk, clerk of the Earlham College faculty, offers this analysis: "When people say that consensus decision-making is a papered-over version of voting they either don't understand what they are observing or the group is not functioning in a consensus-building mode. If the person is party to a consensus decision-making process, the difference will be understood. Because the process is cerebral it is hard to see people's attitudes changing and if the process is not crisply handled, I can easily imagine the judgment that the process is papered-over voting."

Conclusion

The consensus-building and decision-making approach described in this book is based on a clear set of values, and it is distinctive in several ways from other consensus decision-making approaches. The techniques presented in earlier chapters can be used to establish common ground in groups that use other forms of decision-making.

The opportunity and ability to work together, to develop common ground, and to define collective action for ourselves as a community is a fundamental aspect of a democracy. Deciding together on our common enterprise takes courage, demands confidence in our ability to reach agreement, and requires skills and practice. This both builds and requires commitment to live with the necessary tension between ourselves as individuals and as members of a group or community.

Chapter 11
Quakers and Consensus

Introduction

When you hear the word "Quaker," you might think of the guy with the funny hat on the oatmeal box, or maybe of motor oil. If you live in Pennsylvania, you probably know it's nicknamed "the Quaker state," founded by colonial Quaker William Penn. You also may know of Quakers who were drafted during wartime but served in the Red Cross or as medics instead of as combatants because of their religious beliefs.

By now, you probably also link Quakers with consensus, even if you didn't before you started reading this book. But it's important that you know that this form of decision-making is not something Quakers invented; they've just used it a lot for a very long time and, in doing so, have come upon many valuable insights that can help groups work together effectively.

Historically, consensus is a very old form of democratic decision-making. Although fourth- and fifth-century Athenian officials instituted majority rule and voting, evidence shows that seeking the common good and an ideal of unanimity — what Quakers call being "of one mind" — often prevailed. Until England's civil war of the 1640s, that country's Parliament made

> **Distinctive Features of Quaker-Based Consensus Decision-Making**
> - The role of the clerk in guiding the process
> - Belief in our common humanity
> - Dissent / diversity of thought is valued
> - Search for unity

most of its decisions by a form of consensus (Mansfield, 1983). Some Native American tribes have used it for decision-making in religious matters. And many Japanese businesses use a form of consensus practice (Tomlinson, 1996).

There are several aspects of Quaker-based consensus practice that distinguish it from some other commonly used forms. In some other forms of consensus, the boss or person in charge may serve as the facilitator of the process, but this form relies on a clerk. The clerk is neutral with regard to the content but an ardent advocate for the process. As you have seen in the attitudes and practices chapters of this book, the belief in common humanity that includes the capacity to seek common good is central. Quakers often speak of "that of God" in all of us.

When Friends meet in a worshipful stance to make decisions, the search for unity is guided by a belief in the influence of divine presence. In these meetings the use of silence is intentionally prayerful, and the decision-making process is described as seeking "a sense of the meeting" (Morely, 1993). When Friends and others use Quaker-based practice in groups who may not share these religious beliefs, they may refer to the common good or simply act in a way that they hope will reflect their beliefs. As the examples in the introduction have shown, members of other religious and cultural traditions have found it possible to use Quaker-based consensus.

The ways in which diversity of thought and dissent are valued grow from the belief in the ability of all of us to access divine insight. What distinguishes Quaker-based consensus practice is the Quaker perspective on the tension between the individual and the group. While engaged in seeking consensus, individual Quakers look within to discern "leadings," or guidance from God as to what the group's next step should be. Sometimes, however, leadings of different members conflict — and tension is the obvious result. But instead of proceeding with the assumption that any one person's idea is wrong or right, better or best, Quakers assume that each leading is likely to contain elements of truth. The challenge, then, is not to decide whose ideas "win," but to test these individual leadings in the group and to seek clarity or discernment on a course of action for the group.

In Tension: Group Commitment and Individual Leading

Quakers began to use consensus in the 1650s as a means of church governance as they confronted persecution and imprisonment in England for their religious beliefs and practices. To get a sense of what that was like, imagine for a moment that we are Quakers during those turbulent times.

Imagine that people in our country have been struggling for more than one hundred years with issues of religious freedom. For centuries the popes had been regarded as rulers of all Christendom, and kings and queens were also believed to be divinely chosen. Religious services were tightly scripted in Latin and thus not easily understood by the average citizen or worshiper. The separation we have today between church and state did not exist then. Church bishops usually were the most powerful local officials and were secular princes as well.

As the winds of reform from the European continent reached England, King Henry VIII broke with Rome, establishing the Church of England and opening the way towards Protestantism in England. The Bible became widely available in English. However, creating a new church proved to be almost as challenging as living with the old one. Emerging Protestant England and influx of many new ideas from religious groups such as the Calvinists, Anabaptists, and Lutherans led to particularly English expressions of Protestantism, some conservative and some radical. The Religious Society of Friends arose among this excitement of religious ferment during the period of the Commonwealth when England was briefly without a monarch and there was wide tolerance. When Oliver Cromwell died, the political and religious crisis led to the return of the monarchy and re-establishment of the Anglican Church and efforts to suppress all forms of religious dissent.

If we imagine, then, that we are early Quakers, we would be among the dissenting groups. Because we believe that each of us can look to the light of Christ within us, we do not look to clergy as intermediaries, and we don't need external rites to experience divine guidance. On grounds of conscience we refuse to acknowledge the state-sponsored church, and we would thus also refuse to pay government-imposed tithes to support that church. For this we would face imprisonment and steep fines. Believing that all men and women are equal, women would be ministers, and the men among us would express these beliefs by refusing to remove their hats or bow to authorities. We also would use distinctive forms of speech: the informal "thee" and "thou" with officials who usually commanded the more formal "you." Because we believe simplicity is natural and the dictates of fashion are worldly, we dress simply, in clothes of black, brown or grey with little adornment. And we would meet to worship even though to do so was a severely punishable crime.

These things make us easily identifiable and raise the ire of the officials to whom we refuse to defer. As a result of our actions, many of us are arrested and thrown in jail. While we are in jail, the only way to get food and medical care is through the generosity of our friends. They also must care for our children or other dependents left at home.

In such a context, if one of us has a leading to undertake action, it might result in imprisonment of that Friend, and it could also put others of us in jeopardy. We each benefit from exploring our leading in consultation with others in our group before acting upon it. We benefit as a group from thinking through the consequences the action might have for the group as a whole. That serves two purposes: it helps us clarify what should be done and why, and it allows others to commit to sharing with us the consequences of our actions.

> **Led, Driven or Called?**
>
> To discern whether our thoughts and ideas about actions are truly leadings — more than our own desires or those of others — one Friend phrases some traditional tests for a concern:
>
> - What is the community's guidance?
> - What is the gathered wisdom of historical practice and belief?
> - What is the Biblical witness?
> - Can I be patient in deciding? (Self is often impatient, but true leading isn't.)
> - Does it make demands on others but require little of me to carry it out?
> - Whom does it serve?
>
> Paul Lacey, Earlham College professor

Individual Leadings to Test the Group

Because Quakers value both individual leadings and commitment to the group, it's no surprise that their decision-making process offers no simple rule for resolving the tension between these perspectives on all issues. It is precisely this tension that helps draw us into a deeper search for the truth in deciding what is the right action in a given situation.

The story of John Woolman, a New Jersey Quaker born in 1720, illustrates the importance of an individual challenging the group to explore its truth. Drawing on his religious beliefs and leading, Woolman became clear that the practice of slavery was harmful not only to those living in bondage but to the slaveholders' spiritual life. He went to the South to gain first-hand experience, then visited slave-owning Quakers and tried to persuade them to free their slaves. He spoke at Quaker business meetings and wrote treatises on the subject.

Although some Quakers easily came to appreciate his view, others did not. It took decades, but he finally was successful. By the time of the American Revolution, Quakers could be disowned for owning or trading slaves, long before our nation would erupt into war over the issue (Moulton, 1973).

Some Features of Quaker Worship Reflected in Consensus

Quakers' consensus process also is distinguished by present-day worship traditions that grow out of their religious beliefs, many of which date back to the early Quakers who believed in equality, integrity, simplicity, and peace-making. Although Quakers no longer dress like the guy on the oatmeal box (or his wife, who was surely just as plainly dressed), many still ignore the whims of fashion and wear simple, functional clothing. Few say "thee" or "thou" except as a nostalgic way of acknowledging with other Quakers their shared religious heritage, but they still believe in equality and seek to find ways to express that conviction that meet the needs of modern society. And, after centuries of experience with consensus, they still believe that by putting aside personal predispositions and being open to divine guidance, a group can reach corporate discernment based on the collective experience of the presence of God.

The photo below shows the traditional way Quaker meetinghouses are set up. What do you observe about this space that might reflect the way people who draw on the Quaker tradition might govern themselves?

Stout Meetinghouse at Earlham College, a Quaker college in Richmond, Indiana. Meetings for worship and faculty meetings both are held in this room.

Each meeting begins with a period of silence, a practice that goes back to the mid-1600s as a central aspect of worship. The silence provides a time for attenders to quiet themselves so that they might be open to being divinely led, individually and corporately.

Here's a summary of some underlying beliefs that are reflected in Quaker worship services, which they call Meetings for Worship, and in the Quakers' way of practicing consensus:

- There is that of God in everyone.

- God can be revealed to anyone and anyone can have access to the truth.

- Everyone in the community has the responsibility to minister to the community.

- The group is responsible for its spiritual life and everyone shares in that responsibility.

- When someone is clear that he or she has something to say from his/her own experience that might speak to the spiritual condition of the group, the member will rise and speak.

- Face-to-face, non-hierarchical relationships provide a context for exploring one's own truth as well as the good of the community.

- Simplicity helps keep one's focus on faithfulness to one's leadings from God.

Quakers Today

Quakers, properly known as The Religious Society of Friends, numbered 281,860 members in 1999. Most are in Kenya (92,672), the United States (92,263), Bolivia (31,000), and Great Britain (17,189). Given the importance of the testimonies on simplicity, equality, integrity and peace-making to Friends, they may be found working for Native American rights, prison reform, racial justice, education, the women's movement, and peaceful resolution of conflicts.

References on Quaker Consensus

Barbour, H. (1964). *The Quakers in Puritan England*. New Haven: Yale University Press.

Bartoo, G. (1978). *Decision by consensus: A study of the Quaker method*. Chicago, IL: Progresiv.

Beck, J. L. (1994). *Deciding together: An exploration of Friends decision making*. Doctorate of Ministry Thesis. Indianapolis, IN: Christian Theological Seminary.

Birkel, M. (1995, January). Some advice from John Woolman on meeting for business. *Friends Journal*, 15-16.

Brinton, H. (1955). *Guide to Quaker practice*. Wallingford, PA: Pendle Hill.

_____. (1952) *Reaching decisions: The Quaker method*. Wallingford, PA: Pendle Hill.

Browne, G. (1984). *Neither majority nor minority*. [Recording] Cambridge, MA: Kindred Spirits Radio.

Doncaster, L. H. (1958). *Quaker organisation and business meetings*. London: Friends Home Service Committee.

Drake, M. C. (1985) Beyond consensus: The Quaker search for God's leading for the group. Friends consultation on discernment. Richmond, IN: Quaker Hill Conference, pp. 20-32.

Hare, A. P. (1973). Group decision by consensus: Reaching unity in the Society of Friends. *Sociological Inquiry 43* (1), 75-84.

Harvey, F.S. (1980). *The use of the Quaker consensus decision-making process in facilitating moral development*. Ann Arbor: University Microfilms International.

Heathfield, M. (1994). *Being together: Our corporate life in the Religious Society of Friends*. London: Quaker Home Service & Woodbrooke College for the Swarthmore Lecture Committee.

Hickey, D.D. (1987). *Unforeseen joy: Serving a Friends meeting as recording clerk*. Greensboro, NC: North Carolina Yearly Meeting of Friends.

Hinshaw, S. B. (1978). *Friendly procedures in local meetings*. Greensboro, NC: North Carolina Yearly Meeting Publications Board.

Jefferson, B.L. (1995). *Consensus as an alternative decision model in higher education*. Claremont, CA: Claremont Graduate School.

Johnson, E.W. (1991). *Quaker meeting: A risky business*. Pittsburgh, PA: Dorrance PublishingCompany.

Lacey, P. A. (1995). Quaker school: Quaker decision-making. Notes. Richmond, IN: Earlham College.

_____. (1985) *Leading and being led*. Wallingford, PA: Pendle Hill.

Louis, M. (1994). In the manner of Friends: Learnings from Quaker practice for organizational renewal. *Journal of Organizational Change Management, 7* (1), 42-60.

Morley, B.. (1993). *Beyond consensus: Salvaging sense of meeting*. Wallingford, PA: Pendle Hill.

Palmer, P. J. (1990). *Leading from within: Reflections on spirituality and leadership*. Indianapolis, IN: Indiana Office for Campus Ministries.

Penn, W. (1976). *Rise and progress of the people called Quakers*. Richmond, IN: Friends United Press.

Pollard, F. E., Pollard, B.E., & Pollard, R.S.W. (1949). *Democracy and the Quaker method*. London: The Bannisdale Press.

Punshon, J. (1986). *Portrait in grey: A short history of the Quakers*. London: Quaker Home Service.

Quaker Hill Conference Center (1984). *Friends consultation on Friends in business: Individual empowerment and corporate effectiveness*. Richmond, IN: Quaker Hill Conference Center.

Selleck, G. A. (1986). *Principles of the Quaker business meeting*. Richmond, IN: Friends United Press.

Sharman, C. W. (1983). *Servant of the meeting: Quaker business meetings and their clerks*. London: Quaker Home Service.

Sheeran, M. J. (1983). *Beyond majority rule: Voteless decisions in the Religious Society of Friends*. Philadelphia, PA: Philadelphia Yearly Meeting of the Religious Society of Friends.

Stanfield, D. (1989). *A handbook for the presiding clerk*. Greensboro, NC: North Carolina Yearly Meeting of Friends Publication Board.

Wilsher, B. (1986). *Quaker organization: A plain person's guide to structure and business meetings in the Religious Society of Friends*. London: Quaker Home Service.

Wilson, L. L. (1977). *Quaker decisionmaking: Adapting the Friends' method for use in nonQuaker organizations*. M.S. Thesis. Cambridge, MA: Massachusetts Institute of Technology.

Woolpy, J. (1985, 12 October). The Quaker meeting. *The Friends Quarterly 23*: 566-70.

More information on contemporary Friends is available through links at www.earlham.edu/~consense.

Appendices:
Tools for Using Consensus

Appendix A
Consensus Practices Checklist

As groups learn consensus-building and consensus decision-making, skills are often developed through the use of role-playing and mock decision exercises. Having a group member observe the process and give feedback is an excellent way to help people become aware of the areas in which they are doing well and the areas in which they need to improve as they gain experience in using consensus.

The following checklist can help in the evaluation of a group's effectiveness by observing how frequently group members use specific behaviors that are essential to the consensus process. Using the checklist enables the observer to give detailed feedback to the group about its strengths in using the process, as well as the areas in which it needs to improve.

While observing a group involved in consensus processes, make note of how seldom or frequently you observe the following behaviors. For behaviors seen frequently, mark closer to the "F." For behaviors that were seldom seen, mark closer to the "S." Make note of specific behaviors you observed. If a situation described below did not occur, write "NA" for "not applicable." The following list is divided into clusters for members of the group, for the facilitator or clerk, and for the group and facilitator or clerk regarding the final decision.

Members of the group are:

S------F   Staying focused on the good of the group and not just their own preferences.

S------F   Accepting that disagreement can be normal and useful.

S------F   Listening actively and accurately.

S------F   Trying to understand *why* a concern or idea matters to another member or what the underlying concern really is.

S------F   Using body language and facial expressions that show they are listening and consider others to be reasonable people.

S------F   Avoiding negative feelings (anger, frustration or criticism) towards an individual.

S------F   Treating differences in ideas and strategies respectfully.

S------F   Waiting until speaker has finished to ask for recognition to speak.

S------F   Leaving silence between speakers.

S------F   Putting forth information in a well-organized, well-reasoned way.

S------F   Speaking only once on a topic until other members are heard.

S------F   Addressing the group rather than a specific person so that there is no debate between individuals.

S------F   Respectfully asking others for their ideas or opinions, facts, or other information to back up their ideas.

S------F   Expressing ideas and opinions that are different than those that have already been heard.

S------F   Offering praise or appreciation for ideas expressed by others.

S------F   Recognizing particular expertise of others.

S------F   Building on other ideas or comments to propose a conclusion
           or new direction.

S------F   Summarizing the discussion, including points of agreement
           and difference.

S------F   Withdrawing earlier statements of concern when new information
           or insights suggest a better way forward.

The Facilitator or Clerk is:

S------F   Identifying who will speak next.

S------F   Promoting relatively equal opportunities to speak so that no one
           dominates the discussion or rambles on.

S------F   Helping the members re-focus on the task at hand.

S------F   Making summarizing statements in order to help move the discussion
           forward within a particular agenda item.

S------F   Asking questions that help draw out a speaker's meaning.

S------F   Keeping the group on topic and task, including consulting
           members about moving on.

S------F   When necessary, calling for silent pauses to restore the group
           to its focus.

S------F   Encouraging others to express contrasting viewpoints.

S------F   Redirecting attention to ideas and information that were previously
           disregarded by the group.

S------F   Asking if enough alternatives have been developed, or if criteria
           for problem solution have been met.

The Group and the Facilitator or Clerk are:

S------F   Proposing a "minute" that states the "sense of the group."

S------F   Asking if this represents the group's understanding.

S------F   Asking for approval of the "minute."

S------F   Reaching an overall decision about what to do.

S------F   Reaching consensus on some specific point and deciding what is to be done next.

Appendix B
Group Dynamics Evaluation Form

Groups can improve their ability to build consensus and reach consensus decisions if they are more aware of the group dynamics that allow certain members to exercise power while keeping certain others marginalized.

Individual members can answer the following questions based on what they saw during a recent meeting. Discussion of responses in small groups can help members see patterns of behavior as others see them.

1. The Room: Physical Distribution of Group Members

a.) Physical arrangement: How are participants arranging themselves in the space? Semicircle? Circle? Participants seated around tables? Theater standing or seating? Other?

_____

_____

_____

_____

b.) Is there anything about this setup that gives one identity or social group an advantage over the other? If so, does anyone take action to rearrange people? Describe: Segregation by sex, race, social or other identity group.

_____

_____

_____

_____

. . . .

Adapted from Catharine Herr Van Nostrand, *Gender-Responsible Leadership*.
Newbury Park: Sage, 1993, pp. 254-256.

c.) Are a few (or all) members of one identity or social group isolated from the rest of the group? If so, does this segregated arrangement seem to have any effect on group dynamics? If it has an adverse effect, does anyone take initiative to correct the problem?

_____

_____

_____

_____

d.) Space and status: Does any person (besides the facilitator or clerk) occupy a dominant or "power position," such as the center of a cluster that "takes charge," at the head of a conference table, at the center of a semicircle, behind the podium, or writing on the chalkboard? Does anyone try to control group process by (a) standing when she or he could be sitting, or (b) taking up extra space, such as placing an arm over the back of another person's chair, or putting feet up on another's desk? If so, what is the sex, race, social or other identity group of this member?

_____

_____

_____

_____

_____

e.) Issues of proximity: Does anyone try to "cozy up" to those who take charge by crowding around her or him, by choosing the front row, addressing those in charge frequently, or sitting directly opposite the facilitator or clerk at a table? Conversely, do any persons try to exercise control from a distance, such as withdrawing to a back row or a corner of the room? What is the sex, race, social or other identity group of these individuals who want to either endear themselves to or detach themselves from the facilitator or clerk and the rest of the group? How does their attachment / detachment affect the group's power dynamics?

_____

_____

_____

_____

_____

. . . .

Adapted from Catharine Herr Van Nostrand, *Gender-Responsible Leadership*. Newbury Park: Sage, 1993, pp. 254-256.

f.) Add your own observations. Is there anything else that concerns you about the physical layout of the room or the way participants take up space?

_____

_____

_____

_____

2. The Group Itself: Gender Balance, Social or Other Identity Group, Rapport, and Other Considerations

a.) Group's purpose and history: What is this group's purpose — why are people together? Is this a one-time-only session, a regular meeting, or part of a series? If it is an ongoing group, how long has it been functioning?

_____

_____

_____

_____

_____

b.) Group composition and gender and other dimensions of identity group balance:

_____

_____

_____

_____

List numbers of (or percentages of): females _____ males _____

Other social or identity groups (Name them and give numbers; give exact figures, if possible):

_____

_____

_____

_____

Adapted from Catharine Herr Van Nostrand, *Gender-Responsible Leadership*. Newbury Park: Sage, 1993, pp. 254-256.

c.) If group composition is "skewed" and one sex or other identity group is vastly outnumbered (thereby becoming "token females" or "token males"), how do these tokens act, and how are they treated? Do they tend to isolate themselves? Are they singled out because of their minority status and either overchallenged or underchallenged? Do others make assumptions about them? (For example, "She's the only woman on our committee — let her be secretary and take notes.")

_____

_____

_____

_____

_____

d.) Cliques: Are there any couples, partners, or people who are close friends or coworkers? To avoid the formation of cliques, and to enhance a more balanced process, should these pairs be separated? If the facilitator or clerk does separate pairs, how is this accomplished? (For example, people could be asked to sit next to someone they do not know.) If reshuffling takes place, is this request made at the beginning of the session or later? Do partners react positively or negatively to the request?

_____

_____

_____

_____

_____

_____

e.) Rapport: What sort of rapport or "group spirit" appears to develop? Assess the trust level. Do members seem wary of each other or comfortable together? Is there an obvious feeling of teamwork?

_____

_____

_____

_____

_____

. . . .

Adapted from Catharine Herr Van Nostrand, *Gender-Responsible Leadership*. Newbury Park: Sage, 1993, pp. 254-256.

f.) Status and power differentials: Are you aware of any preexisting status or power differentials that could cause some participants to feel less confident and even intimidated? (For example, a group might contain experienced professionals and a few college-aged students, or high-status male administrators and lower-status female support staff.) If marked differences exist, what effect do they have on who chooses to (or refuses to) participate?

_____

_____

_____

_____

_____

g.) Other demographics: Besides issues of history, gender, and status, should other factors, such as age, race, ethnicity, physical disability and social group, be considered? For instance, are any participants differently abled? Are there members of a linguistic minority — less fluent in the language of the majority? How might these additional factors influence the process?

_____

_____

_____

_____

3. What could you do to make the group work more effectively?

_____

_____

_____

_____

4. Your additional observations:

_____

_____

_____

Adapted from Catharine Herr Van Nostrand, *Gender-Responsible Leadership*. Newbury Park: Sage, 1993, pp. 254-256.

Appendix C

The Use of Electronic Mail
in the Consensus Process
of Decision-Making

by Thomas G. Kirk, Jr.

Electronic mail, or e-mail, is a convenient way for members of a group to communicate. It may even be used to make routine or procedural decisions. E-mail can be used to support a decision-making process that is based on consensus-building and this chapter explores how e-mail might be used in support of such group decision-making. E-mail can also be misused, and when it is, it frustrates the group participants and undermines their sense of membership in group decision-making. This chapter therefore also explores the most critical aspects of e-mail use which the group should explore and agree upon, in order to use e-mail effectively.

E-mail is no substitute for face-to-face meetings in which consensus is sought. This assertion is made because of the nature of the consensus-building process. E-mail might work satisfactorily in reaching consensus on such matters as approval of minutes of previous meetings, setting meeting times and agenda, and responding to largely procedural and routine business. However, procedures for handling group business must be able to deal with the most difficult of decisions which occur when a group starts with significant differences of opinion among members. The consensus model of decision making places a strong emphasis on *the process* in which individuals come together and seek a common ground. It is highly unlikely that individuals laboring independently in busy work settings can achieve a sufficient level of centeredness and understanding of *all* the group members concerns so that a common ground for a decision can be reached via e-mail. The face-to-face meeting provides an environment in which processes of multiple interpersonal reactions can be shared by all. The building of these personal bonds and finding the common ground on which members agree are essential to achieving consensus. These goals are not likely to be achieved through the use of e-mail.

Nevertheless, e-mail can play an effective role in the overall processes of decision-making by a group. There are three types of e-mail use that might be integrated into group decision-making processes. The first of these is non-interactive and is limited to the distribution of documents such as agenda, minutes, and written reports. This type of e-mail requires no response from group members and extends the lead time for distributing printed copies of documents. However, when e-mail is used for these purposes, there is a need to agree on protocols. These protocols are addressed in Section V of the queries below.

A second type of e-mail depends on group interaction and is focused on non-substantive issues. This includes such matters as setting a meeting time, gathering and organizing the agenda, and review of minutes.

A third type of e-mail allows for full interaction among the group for the purpose of exploring business to come before a face-to-face meeting of the group. Electronic communication allows members of the group to participate in a discussion over a longer period of time than a meeting with its fixed time period can allow. Individuals can contribute when they are ready and have time to formulate a response. For those who are reticent to speak in groups, e-mail provides an opportunity to share ideas.

In our non-computerized ways of doing business, there are a whole host of conventions that have grown up over the years. These conventions grease the wheels of doing business because all members of the group know them. Thus, for example, we know when or how agendas get distributed. We know how to respond in face-to-face meetings, and how the consultation, formal and informal, occurs between meetings. However, because there is a lack of experience in using electronic communication processes, and therefore few conventions, the group must establish ground rules and regularly check to see that the ground rules (i.e., processes) are comfortable for everyone. The group must achieve consensus on how e-mail is to be used in its decision-making processes.

To help groups decide how they will use e-mail in their decision-making process, the following queries are offered as points for discussion within the group. Along with the queries are some comments of advice based on experience that may assist the group in its thinking.

I. Do all members of the group feel comfortable with the use of e-mail in the support of group decision-making processes? Are any members of the group concerned that e-mail communication will have untoward effects on the consensus-building process?

    The first concern must be the attitudes of group members toward e-mail. If there is objection to the use of e-mail, then the group must talk about these objections and come to some clearness about how to respond to those objections. Like all other decisions built on consensus, there must be clearness in the group that it is appropriate to use e-mail as part of the group decision-making processes.

    There is not a sufficient body of experience with the use of e-mail to know how its use might affect the quality of the decision-making process. However, it is highly likely that group members' reservations will undermine the opportunity to use e-mail effectively.

    Like other technologies, e-mail may engender fears in group members who have not used it regularly. Therefore, a decision to implement the use of e-mail perhaps cannot be answered without the answers to questions about how e-mail will be used. It may, therefore, be appropriate to return to the question of whether it will be used at all after the 'hows' are explored. A trial period in which use is limited to certain non-interactive processes (e.g., announcing a meeting, distributing agenda, minutes and reports) might be an appropriate way for people to gain experience.

Levels of use might gradually be varied to include such interactive tasks as calling for agenda items and corrections of the minutes before moving to more intensive forms of interaction and sharing.

II. Do all members of the group have access to e-mail on the same basis? If not, are members willing to move forward despite these differences? What can be done to reduce the gaps in the level of access to e-mail?

Participants must all have ready access to e-mail and they should feel comfortable in using it. Being disenfranchised by lack of adequate access and low skill level can isolate group members and make them ineffective participants in the face-to-face meetings.

While the ideal is for every group member to have a personal terminal or computer readily handy at their work location, that is not always possible and alternative methods of access will need to be developed. This will be particularly true in organizations and groups with low levels of technology. At a minimum, individuals need sufficient access so that group members can check their e-mail regularly. How often likely depends on how active the group is, the intensity of the decision-making, and the way in which e-mail is used in the decision-making processes. In early stages when e-mail use is limited to one way communication of documents, then individuals need access to e-mail only once or twice a week. However, if the use of e-mail is heavy and matters requiring decisions are complex, then daily, even several times a day, access may be necessary.

III. How will e-mail be used? For example, can e-mail be used to:

   A. Set the meeting time for the face-to-face meeting?

   B. Distribute the agenda and documents relevant to the agenda?

   C. Distribute meeting minutes?

   D. Call for agenda items?

   E. Elicit questions about the content of agenda items and documents, and call for additional information, the absence of which might stymie initial face-to-face discussion?

   F. Facilitate discussion that will clarify issues and provide presenters of the agenda item with a sense of the concerns of group members?

   G. Report actions taken as a result of decisions in the face-to-face meeting?

   H. Formulate and distribute preliminary minutes of the group's decision?

   I. Review and correct meeting minutes prior to approval at the next meeting?

The questions about types of uses of e-mail listed above are deliberately arranged to represent shifting and intensifying involvement of e-mail in decision-making processes. In questions A through C, the communication is one way, generally from the facilitator (clerk) or other designated leader, to the members of the group. Such uses do not require response from other group members. Questions D and E expect interaction among members of the group, but primarily serve to clarify or collect information.

Questions F through I are uses of e-mail that are part of the decision-making processes that are carried on outside the meeting. In the case of F and G, the activities will largely be discussion in order to understand the details of a proposal or issue and the implementation of decisions. Activities in question H are preliminary steps in the decision-making process, and could, in cases of routine decision-making, be sufficient.

IV. What is to be the relationship between e-mail processes and the formal face-to-face meeting?

    A. What is the relationship between e-mail documents and the typical documentation of a face-to-face meeting? E.g., minutes or other documents derived from a meeting.

        1. Should there be a central repository of e-mail communication?

        2. What is the status of e-mail messages as official documents of the group?

    B. Are participants expected to have copies of e-mail at face-to-face meetings?

    C. How are documents that are subject to discussion to be distributed? Should they be distributed electronically with each person responsible for making their copy, or should hard copies be distributed to all prior to the meeting?

As the face-to-face group meetings become increasingly dependent on the preliminary work done on e-mail, the group needs to develop a clear sense of how what occurs on e-mail should be brought into the face-to-face meeting. This issue becomes an important group process issue for the group leaders. Norms of expectation about the responsibilities of leadership and group members need to be developed and talked about. Failures can occur because there is not a clear understanding of the respective roles of group members. Such failures result in members of the group not being integrated into the processes that e-mail supports and thus weakens group processes.

V. What are the group's expectations for conventions of practice that individuals should follow?

In addition to the queries below, the decision-making group should review general rules of Internet etiquette (see Supplement) and agree whether any of these are appropriate guidelines to follow.

    A. How quickly are individuals expected to respond to posted messages?

        Because e-mail has tended to imply a rapidity or urgency, there can develop a strong sense of guilt or blame if responses do not come immediately. Just as we allow time in the face-to-face meeting for people to speak, we must do the same with e-mail.

    B. What lead time will be provided for distribution of documents needed for a meeting? Who is responsible for having copies of documents at meetings?

C. What form(s) of salutation and closing in the message are appropriate or needed?

   The header information in an e-mail message can usually be decoded to determine who sent the message and to whom (individuals or group). Therefore, a salutation and "signature" are not essential. However, the group may prefer certain information in the body of the message to make it easier to identify who the mail is from and who was to receive it.

D. How should reference be made to earlier pieces of e-mail and to threads of ideas? (e.g., Does responder repeat the earlier message, or a part of the message to provide orientation for her/his comments? How much of the prior thread of the conversation gets carried forward in each message?)

E. Is it expected that all group business messages will be distributed to the entire group? Are messages to individuals or subgroups appropriate? Are all messages of a group public information within the group?

F. How public is group information outside the group?

G. As part of group communication, when should responses be sent to individuals as opposed to the entire group? If a listserv is established for the group, will the software default to distributing a response to the group or an individual?

Earlier, the comment was made that significant procedural conventions are used in traditional non-mediated communication to support the decision-making process. Because this traditional process is generally well known to group participants, the traditional processes are taken for granted. However, the expanding use of e-mail and other electronic information can lead to confusion and have an untoward effect on team building goals. It is therefore important that procedures are agreed upon. These procedures are the etiquette of e-mail discourse and by adherence to an agreed upon set of procedures, individuals can make communication meaningful, while not offending group members.

Supplement to
"The Use of Electronic Mail in the Consensus Process of Decision-Making"

Electronic Communications

(E-mail, LISTSERV groups, Mailing lists, and Usenet)

(From "The Net: User Guidelines and Netiquette"
by Arlene Rinaldi)

Under United States law, it is unlawful "to use any telephone facsimile machine, computer, or other device to send an unsolicited advertisment" to any "equipment which has the capacity to transcibe text or images (or both) from an electronic signal received over a regular telephone line onto paper." The law allows individuals to sue the sender of such illegal "junk mail" for $500 per copy. Most states will permit such actions to be filed in Small Claims Court. This activity is termed "spamming" on the Internet.

- Never give your userID or password to another person. System administrators that need to access your account for maintenance or to correct problems will have full priviledges to your account.

- Never assume your e-mail messages are private nor that they can be read by only yourself or the recipient. Never send something that you would mind seeing on the evening news.

- Keep paragraphs and messages short and to the point.

- When quoting another person, edit out whatever isn't directly applicable to your reply. Don't let your mailing or Usenet software automatically quote the entire body of messages you are replying to when it's not necessary. Take the time to edit any quotations down to the minimum necessary to provide context for your reply. Nobody likes reading a long message in quotes for the third or fourth time, only to be followed by a one line response: "Yeah, me too."

- Focus on one subject per message and always include a pertinent subject title for the message, that way the user can locate the message quickly.

- Don't use the academic networks for commercial or proprietary work.

- Include your signature at the bottom of e-mail messages when communicating with people who may not know you personally or broadcasting to a dynamic group of subscribers.

- Your signature footer should include your name, position, affiliation and Internet and/or BITNET addresses and should not exceed more than 4 lines. Optional information could include your address and phone number.

- Capitalize words only to highlight an important point or to distinguish a title or heading. Capitalizing whole words that are not titles is generally termed as SHOUTING!

- *Asterisks* surrounding a word can be used to make a stronger point.

- Use the underscore symbol before and after the title of a book, i.e. _The Wizard of Oz_.

- Limit line length to aproximately 65-70 characters and avoid control characters.

- Never send chain letters through the Internet. Sending them can cause the loss of your Internet Access.

- Because of the international nature of the Internet and the fact that most of the world uses the following format for listing dates, i.e. MM DD YY, please be considerate and avoid misinterpretation of dates by listing dates including the spelled out month. Example: 24 JUN 96 or JUN 24 96

- Follow chain of command procedures for corresponding with superiors. For example, don't send a complaint via e-mail directly to the "top" just because you can.

- Be professional and careful what you say about others. E-mail is easily forwarded.

- Cite all quotes, references and sources and respect copyright and license agreements.

- It is considered extremely rude to forward personal e-mail to mailing lists or Usenet without the original author's permission.

- Attaching return receipts to a message may be considered an invasion of privacy.

- Be careful when using sarcasm and humor. Without face-to-face communications your joke may be viewed as criticism. When being humorous, use emoticons to express humor. (Tilt your head to the left to see the emoticon smile :-) = happy face for humor.)

- Acronyms can be used to abbreviate when possible, however messages that are filled with acronyms can be confusing and annoying to the reader.

  Examples:
  IMHO= in my humble/honest opinion   FYI = for your information
  BTW = by the way   Flame = antagonistic criticism

References

Filipczak, B. (1996, February). The soul of the hog. *Training*, pp. 38-42.

Gastil, J. (1993). *Democracy in small groups*. Philadelphia: New Society Publishers.

Geber, B. (1992, June). Saturn's grand experiment. *Training*, p. 27.

Greenleaf, R. K. (1987, April 27). *Consensus decision-making* [video available at Earlham Quaker Foundations of Leadership, Earlham College, Richmond, IN]. Newton Center, MA: The Robert K. Greenleaf Center.

Harvey, J. B. (1988). The Abilene Paradox: The management of agreement. In *The Abilene paradox and other meditations on management*. Lexington, MA: Lexington Books.

Hunton, J. E., Price, K. H., & Hall, T. W. (1996, December). A field experiment examining the effects of membership in voting majority and minority sub-groups and the ameliorating effects of postdecisional voice. *Journal of Applied Psychology*, pp. 806-812.

Kaner, S., with Lind, L., Toldi, C., Fisk, S., & Berger, D. (1996). *Facilitator's guide to participatory decision making*. Gabriola Island, BC: New Society Publishers.

Korsgaard, M. A., Schweiger, D. M., & Sapienza, H. J. (1995, February). Building commitment, attachment, and trust in strategic decision-making teams: The role of procedural justice. *Academy of Management Journal 38*, pp. 60-84. DIALOG (R) file 75: IAC Management Contents (R) 1997 Info. Access Co., 00177711 Supplier Number 16640090.

Landre, B., & Knuth, B. (1993, July-September). Success of citizen advisory committees in consensus-based water-resources planning in the Great Lakes Basin. *Society and Natural Resources*, pp. 229-257.

Larrabee, A. (1993, February 5-7). Clerking: Serving the community with joy and confidence [Pendle Hill Workshop]. Pendle Hill, PA.

Mansbridge, J. (1980). *Beyond Adversary Democracy*. Chicago: University of Chicago.

Moulton, P. P. (1973) *The living witness of John Woolman*. Wallingford, PA: Pendle Hill Publications.

Punshon, J. (1986). *Portrait in Grey: A short history of the Quakers*. Quaker Home Service, London.

Price, K. H., Hunton, J. E., Hall, T. W., Coalter, T. M., & Clinton, D. B. (1997, August). Differential reactions to majority voting procedures and amelioration of voting minority member responses. Academy of Management. Cincinnati, OH.

Schweiger, D. M., Sandberg, W. R., & Ragan, J. W. (1986). Group approaches for improving strategic decision making: A comparative analysis of dialectical inquiry, devil's advocacy, and consensus. *Academy of Management Journal, 29*, pp. 51-71.

Sheeran, M. J. (1983). *Beyond majority rule: Voteless decisions in the Religious Society of Friends*. Philadelphia: Philadelphia Yearly Meeting.

Susskind, L., McKearnan, S., & Thomas-Larmer, J., eds. (1999). *The Consensus Building Handbook: A Comprehensive Guide to Reaching Agreement* (L. Susskind, S. McKearnan, & J. Thomas-Larmer, Eds.). Thousand Oaks, CA: Sage.

Tomlinson, S. (1996). Comparison of Consensus Japanese Style and Quaker Style. A paper prepared for completion of an independent study in Management. Richmond, IN: Quaker Foundations of Leadership, Earlham College. Accessed at http://www.earlham.edu/~consense/scott2.shtml, [2000, July 16].

Vroom, V. H., & Jago, A. G. (1988). *The new leadership: Managing participation in organizations*. Englewood Cliffs, NJ: Prentice-Hall, Inc.

Tom Strickland

From left: Trayce Peterson,
Cheryl Gibbs, Susan Hillmann,
and Joanna Schofield

Paul Mays

Monteze Snyder and George Watson

About Earlham

Earlham College is an undergraduate, residential college providing the highest quality education in the liberal arts, including the sciences. Drawing students from across the United States and many foreign countries, the education it provides is shaped by the distinctive perspectives of the Religious Society of Friends (Quakers).

The Earlham School of Religion is a Quaker seminary that prepares men and women of all branches of Friends and other traditions and faiths for leadership that empowers and equips the ministry of others.

Both Earlham College and the Earlham School of Religion are located in Richmond, Indiana. Both are deeply grounded in the beliefs and practices of the Religious Society of Friends (Quakers). These Quaker roots are not just history or heritage, but a living, vital connection. The Institute for Quaker Studies, which serves both Earlham College and the Earlham School of Religion, seeks to integrate our Quaker resources both on campus and in relation to the wider Religious Society of Friends.

Conner Prairie is a living history museum located in Fishers, Indiana, north of Indianapolis. First established by Eli Lilly, Conner Prairie is now organized as a wholly owned subsidiary of Earlham. It provides a variety of authentic, unique and entertaining educational experiences that show how America developed.

For more information, call or visit one of our Web sites:

Earlham College
1-800-EARLHAM
www.earlham.edu

Earlham School of Religion
1-800-966-1836
www.earlham.edu/~esr/

Institute for Quaker Studies
1-765-983-1413

Conner Prairie
1-800-432-1377
www.connerprairie.org